Nobility of Spirit

Nobility of Spirit
A FORGOTTEN IDEAL

Rob Riemen

Translated by Marjolijn de Jager

Foreword by George Steiner

Yale University Press • *New Haven & London*

Publication has been made possible with financial support from the Foundation for the Production and Translation of Dutch Literature.

Designed by Nancy Ovedovitz and set in Monotype Perpetua type by Duke & Company, Devon, Pennsylvania. Printed in the United States of America.

Library of Congress Cataloging-in-Publication Data
Riemen, Rob, 1962–
Nobility of spirit : a forgotten ideal / Rob Riemen ; translated by Marjolijn de Jager ; foreword by George Steiner.
p.   cm.
Includes bibliographical references.
ISBN 978-0-300-13690-6 (alk. paper)
1. Nobility of character. I. Title.
BJ1533.N6R56 2008
170—dc22   2007046550

A catalogue record for this book is available from the British Library.

The paper in this book meets the guidelines for permanence and durability of the Committee on Production Guidelines for Book Longevity of the Council on Library Resources.

10 9 8 7 6 5 4 3 2

If you want to understand, really understand the way things are in this world, you've got to die at least once. And as that's the law, it's better to die while you're young, when you've still got time to pull yourself up and start again.

—Giorgio Bassani, *The Garden of the Finzi-Continis*

Contents

Foreword

When Thomas Mann met President Franklin Roosevelt, he was introduced as the "incarnation of European civilization." Mann would not have denied it. As Rob Riemen points out in his loving tribute, there were few aspects of that imperiled civilization which Mann did not embody and express. Though profoundly German in his sensibility and vision, Mann had drawn in his sovereign works not only on the Greek and Latin classics, on the tidal motion of the Bible, on the history of European literature and music, but also, in a series of penetrating essays, on the masters of Russian fiction and drama. Like Goethe himself, his constant model and, in a sense, his hidden rival, Thomas Mann spoke for and of *Weltliteratur.* Riemen evokes this universalism from the center. When catastrophe came, it was only fitting that Thomas Mann should, in the tragic shadow of Luther, of Goethe and of Nietzsche, create what is probably the only work of fiction, *Doctor Faustus,* commensurate with its theme.

What commands Rob Riemen's particular fidelity, however, as well as the ideals of the Nexus Institute, is that particular humanism of which Mann was, perhaps, the last encompassing representative. This humanism Riemen identifies with the complex notion of values. As he suggests, the concept of *time,* of a remembrance of time itself, is crucial, and, as is said in the celebrated opening sentence of the *Joseph and His Brothers* epic, takes man back to the wellsprings of his being. Mann articulates an order in which there is time for reflection, for the cultivation of private consciousness and the mystery of eros (*Death in Venice* can be understood as a single meditation on time suspended). Classical humanistic values, with their philosophic-political sources in Socrates and Plato, privilege the life of the mind. They entail a fundamental trust in the powers, always imperfect but incessantly sustained, of the human spirit in confronting not only personal suffering—Mann is a magic chronicler of illness—but the recurrent pulse of barbarism in history. Of this confrontation Riemen movingly makes of Mann's routine of daily creation an emblem and a lesson.

The analysis and enactment of humanistic values transcends the reach of even individuals of genius. It requires what we might call, in the deepest sense, a *conversazione*. Both in the institute, which he and Kirsten Walgreen established and preside over, and in these meditations, Riemen focuses on conversations. He is rightly fascinated by dialogue and the often somewhat hidden processes whereby insight can emerge from polemic disagreement. He has vividly in mind the Socratic dialogues and symposia as well as the matchless intellectual and emotive debates in Mann's *The Magic Mountain.* As long as language is allowed to prevail, as long as "we can keep talking to each other," there is hope for civility and the pursuit of truth.

The forces now aligned against humanistic values are manifold. As Riemen dramatizes in the last and most shocking of these essays, high culture and enlightened decency offered no protection against totalitarian barbarism. Indeed, eminent thinkers and artists were allies of that barbarism. On an ambivalently positive note, the democratization of current politics, the egalitarian leveling of education, and the dominant place of the mass media militate against that elitism enshrined in Thomas Mann's formula: *Nobility of Spirit*. It is far from certain how and in what context the criteria of excellence that Rob Riemen stands for can flourish. At present, the major energies of the spirit seem manifest in the natural sciences and in technology, modes of human enterprise that differ radically from those in the humanities. Our world is that of Galileo and Darwin. The sphere of the word (Logos), to which these texts address themselves in worried celebration, is shrinking.

This neither diminishes nor falsifies Rob Riemen's reflections. For he is one who, eloquently, believes in the light even before there is dawn.

George Steiner

Prelude: Dinner at the River Café

Who are you indeed who would talk or sing
to America?
—Walt Whitman, *Leaves of Grass*

I

You cannot plan the most important events in your life
—they happen to you. The day that a friendship or a
great love wanders into your life is unanticipated; the
hour that a beloved person departs this life is unanticipated;
the one event that changes your life forever is unanticipated.
At such moments, it is as if—conscious of its power to evaluate
what is and is not truly important, what will remain with you
forever and what you are free to forget—the human soul au-
thorizes the part of you that remembers to carefully record,
with all the senses activated, every detail that the soul will
subsequently make its own. Our brains are good for dates and
facts that can be forgotten when no longer needed. But nothing
that is safely stored in our hearts will ever be lost. This is very
simply but strikingly portrayed in the Hollywood classic *When
Harry Met Sally:* Just ask an elderly married couple when they
first met, and with surprising accuracy they remember details

that are fifty, sixty years old. They have forgotten many things but not that first encounter, etched in their hearts.

II

There was no reason for me to expect anything out of the ordinary from my November 2001 trip to several American cities and universities. A fascinating aspect of my work for the Nexus Institute is meeting with the internationally famous thinkers invited to speak at the annual Nexus Conference, always on a cultural-philosophical topic, and discussing the content of their lecture or panel topic with them. Both the participating speakers and the theme of the upcoming conference—The Quest of Life: Evil—had long been established. That was why, among other reasons, meetings had been scheduled in New York with the Melville scholar Andrew Delbanco; in Chicago with J. M. Coetzee; at Stanford with the Dostoyevsky biographer Joseph Frank and the philosopher Richard Rorty; and in Washington, D.C., with Leon Wieseltier, who had made a deep impression at one of our earlier conferences. The participation of Michael Ignatieff—closely involved with the Nexus Institute from the start—and the historian Daniel Goldhagen provided a welcome reason to revisit Harvard as well. In all likelihood every one of these meetings would be pleasant and interesting. But to expect them to be "unforgettable" would be an exaggeration.

Fortunately, even during a business trip not every appointment has to be work related, and I was eagerly awaiting my dinner with Elisabeth Mann Borgese at the famous River Café in New York on the day of my arrival from Amsterdam. This date, too, had been set in advance, and there was no reason to expect anything more than a pleasant conversation with an old friend. I fear it is a sign of the times that few people are familiar with the identity of Elisabeth Mann Borgese. When I mention her name, the usual reaction is a blank look. More often than not, I add impulsively: "Youngest daughter and beloved child of the great writer Thomas Mann." I realize, however, that this description is really a statement about Mann's importance to me and does no justice to the qualities of his youngest daughter. I do greater justice to Elisabeth when I mention that Al Gore, with his film *An Inconvenient Truth,* is continuing the work that Elisabeth Mann Borgese began.

Because that particular night at the River Café would be so different from what I expected, it makes sense to tell a little more about the woman to whom the existence of this book is largely due.

She was born in Munich in 1918 and was exiled to Switzerland with her parents in 1933; she immigrated to the United States with her parents in 1938 and married the Italian literary scholar, political activist, and celebrated anti-Fascist Giuseppe Borgese. They became the soul of a movement that sought to guarantee peace after the world war was won—a peace that would be accomplished through the creation of a world constitution and a world federation. They could count on the support of such figures as Gandhi, Sartre, Camus, Bertrand Russell, Albert Einstein, and Thomas Mann. In the mid-1960s—her much older husband had died by then—Elisabeth realized that this goal was too utopian for the times. Pragmatically, she decided to dedicate herself to something of greater immediacy— the environment—and realize peace that way.

Elisabeth Mann Borgese was the only female member of the small group that founded the Club of Rome, the first international organization designed to put the environment on the political agenda, to raise humanity's awareness of both the threats to the environment and our shared responsibility to protect it. But even the Club of Rome was not practical enough for her, so she cofounded the International Ocean Institute. This institute devoted itself to upholding a U.N. convention stating that the oceans belong to and are the responsibility of all people and not individual nations. The 1982 acceptance of this proposal by the General Assembly of the United Nations, as well as its ratification in 1994 (without the support of the United States), was primarily due to the efforts of Elisabeth Mann Borgese. She spoke with countless people, and every one of them must have been impressed by her intellect, conviction, and charm.

She was a true embodiment of the twentieth century, counting among her friends Vladimir Horowitz (she had had piano lessons with him in her younger years when she aspired to become a concert pianist), Bruno Walter, Albert Einstein, Jawaharlal Nehru, Indira Gandhi, W. H. Auden, Agnes Meyer, Ignazio Silone, Robert Hutchins, Roger Sessions, and many others. When I first met her, she was eighty years old and living in Halifax, Nova Scotia, where she was working as a professor of international maritime law at Dalhousie University. I had invited her to give the annual Nexus Lecture in the spring of 1999 and had suggested a topic: The Years of My Life. In 1950 her father gave a famous lecture by that title in which he, then seventy-five years old, had looked back on *his* times. It seemed fitting to ask his eighty-year-old daughter to speak about her own times half a century later. Initially she was hesitant: "I do not dare to follow in the footsteps of my father." I managed to persuade her, and on May 12, 1999, in a sold-out hall at Tilburg

University, The Netherlands, with Queen Beatrix and the former prime minister Ruud Lubbers, a friend and a political ally,
in the front row, she delivered an unforgettable lecture. A
friendship was formed, and we kept in touch. When it turned
out that we would both be in New York City in late 2001, we
set a date for dinner: Wednesday, November 7, at 7:30 P.M. at
the River Café.

III

When I jotted down the date in my book, two vastly different things that could not have been foreseen profoundly altered
the circumstances of the dinner.

The first one was 9/11. I will never forget the sight of New
York the evening that I, just arrived from Europe, was walking
through the city to get some exercise after the long flight from
Amsterdam. Two months after that calamitous date the city
of lights was dark, cold, and empty. There was hardly any
traffic, with the exception of a few taxis that could not have
been earning much because the pedestrians, too, had vanished.
Some Dutch friends lived on Wooster Street in Soho, so I
headed there. They weren't home. Then a tourist's impulse
drew me toward West Broadway in the direction of Ground
Zero. I still don't know whether the huge black cloud that I
saw suspended in the distance over Ground Zero was real or
fiction. "The horror! The horror!"—the cry from Joseph Con-
rad's *Heart of Darkness*—pierced my mind, and I turned away.
At Washington Square I flagged down a taxi to take me to the
foot of the Brooklyn Bridge and the River Café.

The first to arrive at the nearly empty restaurant, I sat at the
table by the window with a glass of Chardonnay in my hand

and stared out at the Statue of Liberty as she watched over the city. Dom Salvador's "I'll Be Seeing You," which had never sounded more melancholy, was half heard in the background as I waited for my two guests.

Yes, two. That was the second unexpected thing. A few days before my departure Elisabeth phoned, and after the usual preliminaries, she asked whether I had ever heard of Joseph Goodman.

"Should I have?"

"Actually, he's a very solitary figure, but he's an old friend, and I would very much like him to join us."

"Of course. But if you have a minute, I would appreciate it if you could tell me a bit more about him."

When Elisabeth was young and planning to become a concert pianist, she traveled daily from Princeton to New York, where she took lessons from Isabella Vengerova, a great Russian piano teacher connected with the Curtis Institute in Philadelphia. This woman had another student besides Elisabeth: Joseph Goodman. Joe was three years younger than Elisabeth, also came from Germany, and, it later turned out, had arrived in the United States on the same ship, the *New Amsterdam,* sailing into New York Harbor on September 23, 1938. But Joe was traveling in steerage without his parents, who had stayed behind in Germany and whom he would never see again. Elisabeth dined at the captain's table with her famous parents.

According to Elisabeth, Joe was a brilliant pianist. "You should have heard him play Beethoven's Opus 106," she said. But the young man was as introverted as he was brilliant. Elisabeth, who was attracted to him but also concerned about him, managed to gain his trust. They became very close friends. Then, realizing that she did not possess Joe's talent, and for other reasons, too, she abandoned her dream of becoming a pianist and fell in love with Giuseppe Borgese, thirty-six years her senior, with whom she wanted to achieve her new goal: a world constitution, a world federation, world peace. She told Joe that her marriage wouldn't affect their friendship, but he did not attend the wedding and disappeared from her life.

Many years later, in the late 1960s, she ran into him in a secondhand bookstore in New York City, where he was working as a salesman. Elisabeth, a widow by then, was living and working in Santa Barbara, California, where she directed the Center for the Study of Democratic Institutions—this was before she became involved with the environment. Joe, who had never married, was now devoting his life to his second love, books.

"Have you really given up the piano?" Elisabeth asked.

"I couldn't survive as a pianist, Elisabeth. But I do compose now and then." She asked whether she might see some of his work, but he demurred. "Maybe, although I don't know if it's any good."

Joe liked his new life. It gave him plenty of time to read, and in the bookshop he treasured one collection in particular: the works of the poet Walt Whitman.

"You should know that Walt Whitman means the same thing to him that my father means to you," Elisabeth told me. "But he may be even more obsessed with Whitman than you are with my father."

"Were there books of your father's in the bookshop?"

"Just one, *Doctor Faustus*. And Joe showed me copies of two of my father's lectures: 'On the German Republic' and 'The Coming Victory of Democracy.' Do you have any idea why Joe had those lectures?"

"Let me guess: because your father quotes Whitman in them."

"Yes! The two of you will have so much in common," Elisabeth said. "I'm delighted you will meet."

I told Elisabeth that I would love to see the bookshop, but she said that it no longer existed. In the mid-1970s it closed, and Joe had found other employment. He went back to playing the piano, but on cruise ships that sailed the Pacific near Mexico.

To her amazement, when Elisabeth turned sixty on April 24, 1978, she received two messages in one envelope. Joe had composed a song for her set to a poem by Walt Whitman. There was also the announcement of a daughter's birth. The accompanying note said: "Now all is well. The little girl is beautiful. I feel peace and happiness for the first time in my life."

Even though Joe continued to sail the Pacific and Elisabeth moved to Halifax, they continued to stay in touch. "Okay, so you're looking at the Atlantic and I at the Pacific, but at least we're connected by the oceans," he said when he occasionally phoned. For the first time in forty years, Elisabeth had a sense that he was doing well. He was interested in the work she was doing, and spoke lovingly about his child. Then, early in 1988, he phoned again. His daughter had died at the age of ten of a tropical virus. She had been ill with a very high fever for two weeks, but the doctors couldn't do anything. Joe was devastated, and although Elisabeth had never met the little girl, she felt as though she had lost a child of her own. Two years later Joe moved to New York. His marriage had not withstood the deep depression he was once again suffering. And, as if all that weren't enough, he now had a tic, spasmodic torticollis, which caused him to make continuous, uncontrollable movements with his head so that playing the piano was no longer possible.

To Elisabeth he had said: "Although I want to be near you, I am an American. I cannot live in Canada. I must live in the city of Whitman."

She knew he lived downtown, but he would never tell her where, possibly because he was ashamed of his poverty. Elisabeth didn't even have his phone number; he called her. They used to see each other a few times a year and always at his favorite spot: a certain bench in Central Park near the reservoir. He went there every afternoon to catch some fresh air and often found Emilio Contini, a friend from his bookstore days, there as well. On September 11, 2001, when Elisabeth heard about the attack on the Twin Towers, she was desperate to hear from Joe. When he eventually got through and informed her that he was fine, Elisabeth told him she would be in New York two months later. He said: "Then I would love to see you."

I was moved by Elisabeth's story and appreciated her sharing it with me, but was convinced that my presence at the River Café would be intrusive. Elisabeth insisted: "No, Joe wants to meet you. I would like to see you, too. You *must* come."

IV

The old man who sat down at my table at exactly 7:30 was small and frail and had a beard worthy of his poet-hero. His jacket was threadbare. Joe ordered a beer and, leaning his head close to his shoulder to limit its jerks, took a sip. Sitting across from someone whose head wouldn't stop moving and aware of his life story as recounted to me by Elisabeth, I was briefly at a loss for words. Because my companion, busy trying to drink his beer, said nothing either, I feebly tried to make conversation.

"Have you ever been here before?"

"No."

"The view is great, isn't it?"

"No, I don't think the view is great. Not anymore."

He must have noticed my embarrassment, and added in a friendlier tone: "At least the 'Mighty Woman' is still there. From here she really does offer a great view, and she's a comfort, too."

"The 'Mighty Woman'?"

"Yes, the Statue of Liberty. Don't you know the poem by Emma Lazarus that is engraved on a tablet on the pedestal?

A mighty woman with a torch, whose flame
Is the imprisoned lightning, and her name
Mother of Exiles.

"I'll never forget the morning that I saw her for the first time. Did Elisabeth tell you that we arrived on the same boat?"

"Yes, she did. I have never been to the Statue of Liberty, nor to Ellis Island. But I recently discovered that on April 13, 1909, a distant relative of mine, Isaac Riemen, arrived in New York from Russia. If I have time tomorrow I'm planning to visit Ellis Island to see if I can find out what happened to him."

"I think Ellis Island is still closed. A security measure. . . . What brings you to New York?"

At that moment, Elisabeth came into the restaurant. She was also small and old but with such vitality. We ordered, Elisabeth had her whiskey (Scotch, single malt—her favorite), and I began to describe the upcoming Nexus Conference—the topic, the participants, and some central questions that would be addressed: Whence evil? Why is there so much evil, injus-

tice, and suffering in human existence? Is there a pervasive
answer to Job's plight, or is life ultimately meaningless?

"I have been asked if we chose this topic to be current. But
the topic for the 2002 conference was selected months before,
and we didn't need September 11 to make a conference on evil
topical. The philosophers Kolakowski and Scruton will address
this. Pumla Gobodo-Madikizela, member of the South African
Truth and Reconciliation Commission, will discuss the face
of evil that she has seen; Moshe Halbertal from Israel will
address the question of Job; Mario Vargas Llosa will be back
to discuss *The Feast of the Goat,* which goes to the core of
malevolent political regimes; we will have a brilliant Canadian intellectual, John Ralston Saul, and so on, including the
people I'll meet on this trip. I think it will be an important
conference."

Elisabeth nodded in agreement, but Joe was not convinced.
"As far as I'm concerned, this is precisely what those intellectuals should *not* be doing now. The whole world is busy discussing evil. Besides, what do you think it will accomplish? Will
humanity improve one iota because of it? Why don't you do
something more positive? Organize a conference on *freedom.*
Because that is what those dirty bastards, those necrophiliac
cowards, want to destroy: the Mighty Woman! America is a
great country, and I realized that the very moment I arrived in
September 1938 and first laid my eyes on this impressive lady,
the true symbol of America. Do you remember that day,
Elisabeth?"

"Of course I remember, Joe. I will never forget the day of
our arrival either, the joy of being greeted by your 'Mighty
Woman.' But to be honest, I don't think America is a great
country anymore. When I became a Canadian citizen, I handed

my American passport back of my own volition. This hasn't been my country for a long time. And in my opinion, it's a good thing for Nexus to organize this conference, if only to clarify that lack of freedom has everything to do with the evil within ourselves. Apart from that, one can only hope that September 11 will also make us realize to what extent the West, the United States in particular, is once again unfaithful to its own ideals. How hypocritical we are when it comes to economic interests and foreign policy! Hypocrisy is the result of the greed that has a stranglehold on our society. Marx certainly got that right: capitalism, too, is a destructive force! Not to speak of the stupidity we cultivate, the decadence. Things like that always have consequences."

"So you think what happened on September 11 is okay? You belong to those who argue that we should try to 'understand' why three thousand innocent people were murdered by religious fanatics? As if it's that difficult to understand that these fascists are simply evil."

Joe was so emotional that his head was jolting ever more wildly, and as a result, it became increasingly difficult for him to get food into his mouth. Calmly, her hand on his arm, Elisabeth said: "No, Joe, it's *not* okay, and you know me well enough to realize that I would never justify the murder of innocent people. And I do know that evil exists. I will never forget March 1933. After a holiday in Switzerland with my parents, I went back to school in Munich. During those two weeks Hitler and his Nazis gained total control over Germany. It was a huge shock to see that the teachers were suddenly declaring the exact opposite of what they had stated before we went away. Girls who just three weeks before were swooning over a teacher now reported him because he had forbidden them to begin the lesson with 'Heil Hitler.' In less than three weeks they had all turned into confirmed Nazis. I was almost fifteen, and since then I have had no illusions whatsoever about the evil that lurks inside human beings. But I *also* know that you cannot eradicate evil with bombs and grenades. We're going to have to come up with a better answer than the so-called war on terror."

"I agree, Elisabeth," I said, "but the key questions remain: What next? How to get *beyond* the war on terror?"

Elisabeth and I looked at each other in surprise when Joe, with a calm in his voice that I hadn't heard yet that evening, said: "*I* know what to do. *I* have the answer!"

He took a brown leather folder from a plastic bag, put it on the table, moved a few glasses aside, opened it, and showed us a sheaf of music paper. On the first page in large letters written in a shaky hand it read:

Symphonic Cantata for Solo, Choir and Orchestra

NOBILITY OF SPIRIT

Words of Walt Whitman

by

Joseph Goodman

"This is what I wanted to show you, Elisabeth. Please, have a look."

The work was based on lines from *Leaves of Grass,* a hymn to freedom, democracy, America, and poetry, and began with a recitative and an aria in which New York is celebrated:

I too walk'd the streets of Manhattan island

Give me faces and streets
Let me see new ones every day

The chorus follows:

> People, endless, streaming, with strong voices, passions,
>   pageants,
> Manhattan streets with their powerful throbs, with
>   beating drums as now,
> Manhattan faces and eyes forever for me.

My knowledge of music is limited, but the impression I got
from this rough draft—for it was a draft; the entire score
obviously still in *statu nascendi*—was of Manhattan lauded in
the form of a lamentation. The second part of the work, about
the poet and freedom, was more contemplative and melodic
(*andante grazioso*), written for soprano and orchestra:

> The poets are the voice and exposition of liberty.
> Whatever satisfies the soul is true.
>
> Liberty, let others despair of you
> I never despair of you.
>
> For the great Idea, the idea of perfect and free individuals
> For that, the bard walks in advance, leader of leaders.
>
> For the great Idea,
> That, O my brethren, that is the mission of the poets.

The third and final section, for alto, choir, and orchestra—
with many kettledrums and trombones—was a paean to
America, entitled "So Long!"

> Any period one nation must lead,
> One land must be the promise and reliance of the future.
>
> When America does what was promis'd,

When through these States walk a hundred millions of
    superb persons,
I announce justice triumphant,
I announce uncompromising liberty and equality,
I announce the justification of candor and the justification
    of pride.
I announce splendors and majesties to make all the previous
    politics of the earth insignificant.

I was intrigued, and while Elisabeth, who had far greater
musical expertise than I, was examining the score, I asked Joe
why he had chosen this particular topic.

"Nobility of spirit *is* the great ideal! It is the realization of
true freedom, and there can be no democracy, no free world,
without this moral foundation. Whitman's masterpiece, his
whole vision, is exactly about this: life as a quest for truth, love,
beauty, goodness, and freedom; life as the art of becoming human through the cultivation of the human soul. All this is expressed by 'nobility of spirit': the incarnation of human dignity.
Have you ever read Whitman? No? Then start with his *Democratic Vistas*. It's a brilliant commentary on America and a kind
of philosophical introduction to the poetic vision of *Leaves of
Grass*. Elisabeth is right to be critical of contemporary America.
My America, my great country, is Whitman's vision of America, and his *Vistas* is the best analysis of the gap between the
idea of America and the American reality. Whitman already
knows that a system, political institutions, and the right to vote
are not by themselves sufficient for true democracy. As Whitman claims, the purpose of democracy is that the highest freedom becomes law, and then goodness and virtue will follow.
Political freedom alone is not enough; a different spiritual

climate has to arrive, the era of literature has to emerge. The true poet teaches true freedom. True liberal education is nothing but education in the essence of nobility of spirit. Whitman had the greatest confidence in the spirit of the American people, and so do I. With this work, my music, I want to bring the spirit of Whitman back to life and make the American people aware of their mission in the world.

"Elisabeth," Joe turned to her, "I have never asked a favor of you. But if I can give a new voice to the nobility of spirit, one that will touch the human heart, will you please help me to have it performed? Nobody knows me, but you can make this work. You are known. Will you help?"

I could see in Elisabeth's face how touched she was by the fact that this very proud man who in their sixty-year friendship had never asked for anything or accepted any help from her now sought her support to bring something to life that was of transcendent importance to him. For Joe the work was also an artistic testament, actually the only proof that he had lived on this earth. His parents were dead, his only child was dead, his wife had disappeared, the bookstore had vanished, and during much of his life he had been a voyager on the ocean. With his cantata, his hymn to the nobility of spirit, there would be one work through which he would survive.

Elisabeth kissed his cheek and whispered: "You may count on me."

His pale face deeply flushed, his left hand grimly pushing his head against his shoulder to prevent the violent jolts, he gathered up his pages and prepared to go.

"Why are you leaving?" Elisabeth asked.

"It's Wednesday, and I never miss David Dubal's piano

program on the radio. But thank you, Elisabeth. I'll call you as soon as I have finished it."

"Joe, wait, we can share a taxi!" But he didn't respond. I told him that I wanted to send him my essay on Thomas Mann, and he wrote a post office box number and the name Emilio Contini on a card.

"This is the best way to send me mail. Have a good time in the land of freedom."

He hadn't taken three steps before he turned around and said to me: "I hope there are no footnotes in your text. I hate footnotes!"

I reassured him and he went on his way.

"What's his problem with footnotes?" I asked.

"It's ridiculous. Once, long ago, when he was still trying to make a living as a musician, he was invited to be a guest lecturer in some department of music. I think he had hopes of getting a position, but he made it impossible for himself by not complying with standard academic rules. Ever since then, Joe has considered footnotes the essence of academic absurdity."

Elisabeth had to laugh, but it wouldn't surprise me if she was cheerful about more than her friend's strange dislike of footnotes.

V

Back in the Netherlands at the end of November 2001, I sent Joe the English translation of "The Quest of Thomas Mann," an essay I had published in The Netherlands on the occasion of Elisabeth's Nexus Lecture, as a tribute to what I had learned from her father. I sent it to Joe to say how much I appreciated meeting him and to tell him how much I had enjoyed reading Whitman's *Democratic Vistas*. His poet and my author clearly had much in common, I wrote.

On January 7, 2002, I found a brown envelope in my mail at the Nexus Institute. It contained a used copy (bought at the legendary Strand Bookstore) of Whitman's *Leaves of Grass*. In the now-familiar shaky handwriting Joe had written a dedication: "The American Man. To continue the nobility of spirit." There was a short note with it stating that there was indeed a profound spiritual relationship between Mann and Whitman. And Joe added a comment from Whitman on *Leaves of Grass:* "The true use for the imaginative faculty of modern times is to give vivification to facts, to science and to common lives, endowing them with the glow and glories and final illustriousness which belong to every real thing, and to real things only. Without that ultimate vivification—which the poet and other artists alone can give—reality would seem incomplete and science, democracy, and life itself finally in vain." Joe concluded: "All to say, dear friend, facts are good for scholars, but we must write the truth! Write well, be well. Your friend, Joe."

Later that day, exactly two months after the dinner at the River Café, I called Elisabeth to tell her what I had received in the mail. The moment she answered the phone, I could hear that she was shaken. Elisabeth had been informed only a few hours earlier that Joe had died of a cerebral hemorrhage the previous day. His Italian friend had become concerned when Joe was missing from their regular bench in Central Park and had gone to his home and found him, already dead. Elisabeth had asked Emilio the same question I asked her: "Is the composition finished? Did he complete his *Nobility of Spirit?*" The tragic response was that in a new depressive state, Joe had destroyed all his drafts and notes.

"I am very sorry to hear all this, Elisabeth. My condolences. I appreciate your having introduced me to Joe. He was a great man," I said.

"I don't think he was a *great* man. He was noble, he was a real friend in his own way, and he was a genius, too. Joe always had the most brilliant and original ideas. While he was telling you about Whitman's ideals, I was looking at the draft of his score, and it could have been a masterpiece—a very special blend of his own inspiration with motifs from the works of the masters he so admired. Do you remember the second section? Did you notice that it was a cantilena? I am quite sure that it was partially based on a melody Joe was in love with when we were still studying the piano together: the cantilena from the *Joseph Cantate* by the young Beethoven, a lesser known but magnificent piece of music. The melody is hauntingly beautiful, it gives voice to 'the light,' and Joe uses it to praise the poet who brings freedom, the great Idea, to humanity. What he intended to use for the closing hymn was equally beautiful. It was precisely in that song praising America that he used the motifs from the final part of Brahms's *Altrhapsodie*. That way the music stripped the pathos from the Whitman text. America as the land of freedom and justice was no longer a firm reality but an act of yearning, a profound hope."

"Why did he destroy it all? I don't understand."

"Because, as I said, Joe was *not* a great man. Completing a piece of work requires, as my father always said, 'durchhalten,' 'Ausdauer.' How do you say that in English? Endurance. Perhaps, but that's not really the right translation. Be that as it may, Joe didn't have that kind of character, that strength. He was never able to ward off, or deal with, his own demons. At the same time he was too proud and too fearful to leave behind something that was not great art. And so he ended with nothing, absolutely nothing. . . . Anyway, will you continue his work?"

"I? His *Nobility of Spirit*?"

"Yes. That's what he is asking you to do; that's why he sent you his favorite book: 'to continue the nobility of spirit.'"

"But I do not know how to write music."

"Why music? You're a writer, after all."

"Yes, but I know nothing about Whitman and, unlike Joe, am not even an American."

"This is about more than Whitman and more than America. The horror of September 11, this ghastly beginning of the twenty-first century, should make every living person aware that human dignity is at stake. That is where Joe was completely right, and it is the most important lesson that my century, the twentieth century, taught us. My father once spoke of nobility of spirit as the sole corrective for human history. Wherever this ideal vanishes, culture vanishes with it. You know my father's work. He, too, spent his entire life struggling with this ideal and devoted his most important works to it. Follow his path, trace his steps, let an old ideal become relevant for your time, the twenty-first century."

"I don't know if I can do it."

"Well, you should. And to please Joe: no footnotes! Just some 'poetry' and 'truth.' That would be sufficient even for Goethe." She had to laugh at this herself.

"I'll see. In any event our dinner at the River Café was memorable. I'll never forget it."

"Yes, it was an unforgettable evening. You might even mention it in your book. Give Joe some credit. He deserves it, and then there is at least one place where he will exist."

"The date we met was symbolic as well."

"Symbolic? In what way?"

"During the Renaissance, November 7 was the day that the dates of Plato's birth and death were commemorated. Philosophers would gather to hold a good conversation in the spirit of Plato."

"Well, I guess it's a good thing to be in the Platonic tradition. Anyway, will we meet again in Switzerland to continue our other conversation?"

VI

Elisabeth was planning to go to Switzerland, where she went skiing every year. Kirsten, my wife and partner in the Nexus Institute, and I were also heading for Saint Moritz. Among other things, the almost eighty-three-year-old would teach us how to ski, for she was astonished that we, generations younger than she, didn't know how. I was more interested, however, in the sequel to what she called "our other conversation." After Joe had left the River Café, she had taken a thick, sealed envelope from her bag and said: "This is a surprise. Have a look at it when you're back in your hotel and call me tomorrow."

But the lengthy phone conversation on January 7 turned out to be our last, and Kirsten and I never went to Switzerland. A week before we were due to leave, Elisabeth—who was never ill—suddenly came down with pneumonia. She died on February 8, 2002, in the country where, as a teenager, she had dreamt of a pianist's career and where her parents, Thomas and Katja Mann, had spent the last years of their lives. She, too, is buried in the family tomb in Kilchberg, near the lake of Zurich.

Instead of going to Switzerland, I stayed home and sat in my library, surrounded by Thomas Mann's books and his spiritual universe. My final conversation with Elisabeth in mind, I leafed through Goethe's autobiography, *Poetry and Truth,* then stopped— surely not by coincidence—at the episode in which Goethe describes how in 1824, toward the end of his life, he came upon a letter by the famous German humanist Ulrich von Hutten.

In that letter—written on October 25, 1518, and addressed to a friend, Wilibald Pirckheimer—von Hutten mentions that he doesn't mind being a nobleman but feels that he has to earn the title himself, despite his aristocratic lineage: "It is a form of nobility that rests solely on chance and is therefore worthless to me. I seek the source of nobility elsewhere and will drink from that." The letter is an important document from an era in which (once again) the idea of the *nobilitas literaria* was born: true nobility is the nobility of the spirit. The classics, the sciences, but beauty and form also, exist to ennoble the spirit, to allow human beings to discover their supreme dignity. (Baldassare Castiglione's *Book of the Courtier* and his plea for *sprezzatura* go back to this same period.)

Three centuries later, when Goethe read this letter, he was so profoundly moved by its significance for his own time that he published a large section of it in his autobiography.

I read and reread that part of the letter, but for some reason I wasn't convinced and even noticed a certain irritation with his position rising within me. Nobility of the spirit is an ideal of *knowledge?* In his symphonic cantata could Joe have been interested in a form of *knowledge?* Was it a sixteenth-century ideal of *knowledge* that Elisabeth believed should become relevant to the twenty-first century? Her father's work had taught me the importance of *Bildung,* but the great writer was also intimately familiar with betrayal by the very people who possessed considerable knowledge: the intellectuals. No, nobility of spirit had to be more than a sixteenth-century ideal of knowledge. Joe knew that, Thomas Mann knew that, and I would have understood that Goethe knew it as well had I started at the beginning of his autobiography, for he learned very early on what the essence of nobility of spirit was, thanks to a single book, *Ethica,* by the Dutch Jewish philosopher Baruch de Spinoza. In this 1677 work about God, human nature, and the human spirit, Goethe found a convincing answer to his questions about true happiness, the true meaning of freedom, and the right way to live. For Goethe, the power of this book lay not merely in the argument, articulated with mathematical precision and clarity, but in the fact that its author had managed to shape his own life in accordance with his strict, high-minded life principles.

Everything that Goethe wrote about Spinoza quickly made it clear to me that Joe's "Mighty Woman," the Statue of Liberty that had greeted him and Elisabeth upon their arrival in New York, was the spiritual daughter of the Dutch philosopher. "Follow the path!" Elisabeth had told me. It was not in New York, nor in Switzerland, nor in Germany, but in my own country, the Netherlands, that I began to pursue in earnest a *forgotten ideal of life.* I spent the following weeks reading the work of the man who to such a great extent had made the nobility of spirit his own.

VII

Baruch de Spinoza is twenty-four years old when he abandons the trade milieu in which he has been raised in order to devote the rest of his life to the quest for truth and the pursuit of living in truth. Why? In *On the Improvement of the Understanding*—a brief, unfinished treatise that can be read as a preliminary study for his *Ethica*—he explains his choice: Experience has taught him that almost everything in life is vain and trivial. Inevitably the question arises whether there isn't some true and lasting good within the grasp of human beings such that they might live good and true lives. The young man is perfectly aware that *this* kind of life signifies a radical break with a society in which everyone is guided by the hunger for "wealth, honor, and sensual pleasure." Yet he has already noticed that these desires can never bring permanent happiness and peace of mind. Moreover, he has already had the experience that even concentrated thinking, the attempt to understand what truth and the right way to live are—however ephemerally—brings him the calm and joy he seeks. This almost physical experience, as simple as it is essential, provides Spinoza with two insights that determine the rest of his life.

The mind is the greatest gift humanity possesses. By thinking for *oneself*, anyone can become familiar with what is truly and lastingly good and live accordingly. The best life is thus wholly devoted to thought, to the love of wisdom. In a letter to a friend Spinoza confesses: "Let everyone live according to his personal inclinations as long as I can live for truth." At the same time, he realizes that truth and freedom are always entwined. Anyone who is not free cannot live in truth. The ban that the Jewish community of Amsterdam imposes on him—not

merely because of his ideas but also because of his attitude toward life—is an additional form of liberation for Spinoza, that
is, liberation from the oppression of religious fanaticism, where
thinking independently is not allowed, backwardness is upheld,
and hatred for those who think differently is cultivated. As
Spinoza learns not long thereafter, these constraints are part
of every form of fundamentalism.

Set free from the power of religion and money, he will here-
after "live for truth and for freedom," and he will never again
be unfaithful to either.

The invitation from a German Elector to accept the position
of professor of philosophy in an illustrious academy guarantees
him money, prestige, and power. The invitation includes a
promise: "You will have ample freedom to philosophize, but
we trust that you will not abuse this to disturb the religion
established by the state." Spinoza courteously but firmly lets
him know by return mail that he will not accept the distinguished offer. He knows that a professorship could only thwart
his efforts to achieve his life's goal. True thinking requires
independence. Power and money—as paradoxical as it may
seem—are nothing but restrictions on this freedom.

However, Spinoza is not merely interested in his own
happiness. On the contrary, he believes that those who strive
for what is truly good cannot rejoice in the unhappiness of
others. Besides, a society in which truth and freedom are not
recognized will ultimately cease to exist. He demonstrates
with his *Ethica* that true happiness can exist only in wisdom
and knowledge about truth, and that knowledge that can be
attained only through the human intellect. Still, the prejudices,
intolerance, and hatred of the powerful theologians and
preachers keep him from publishing the work during his

lifetime. He does publish his *Theologico-Political Treatise,* if under a pseudonym. Here he argues that political freedom is a basic condition for a society in which people can find true happiness. He summarizes the essence of his treatise on the title page of his book: "Containing a number of dissertations, wherein it is shown that freedom to philosophise can not only be granted without injury to Piety and the Peace of the Commonwealth, but that the Peace of the Commonwealth and Piety are endangered by the suppression of this freedom." Freedom of thought, freedom of opinion, and tolerance must be the purpose of politics. This is of equal importance to the state itself: "What greater misfortune for a state can be conceived than that honorable men should be sent like criminals into exile because they hold diverse opinions which they cannot disguise?" Spinoza therefore concludes, in this 1670 work, that democracy is the form of government that best safeguards this freedom.

Less than two years later, on August 20, 1672, the brothers Johan and Cornelis de Witt, leaders of the Republic of The Netherlands, are murdered in The Hague. Goaded by Calvinist preachers, the perpetrators are supporters of the Prince of Orange who hang the brothers from a gallows by their feet, cut off their body parts, and sell these as souvenirs. Spinoza, who is a great admirer of Johan de Witt and knows that he owes his own relative political freedom to the existence of the republic, is appalled. He rarely lets his emotions get the better of him, but now, as an inhabitant of The Hague, he wants to go to the spot where the murder took place and post a placard with just two words: "Ultimi barbarorum." His landlord prevents him from going out and locks the door. The bloodthirsty mob would surely have killed the freedom-loving philosopher as well.

What is the future of democracy, of political freedom, if people no longer know what the essence of freedom is? When they no longer think, no longer let themselves be guided by reason, but are enslaved by superstitions, fears, and desires?

The final section of *Ethica* substantiates one of the most important insights that Spinoza owes to his philosophical work and life. The essence of freedom, he teaches, is nothing more than dignity itself. Only those who know how to comply with the call to be human, only those who won't allow themselves to be possessed by desire, wealth, power, or fear but instead manage to make their own that which is lastingly and truly good and allow freedom and truth to guide them—only they know the true meaning of freedom. Spinoza concludes *Ethica* with these stirring words: "If the way which I have pointed out as leading to this result seems exceedingly hard, it may nevertheless be found. How would it be possible, if salvation were ready to our hand, and could without great labor be found, that it should be by almost all men neglected? *Sed omnia praeclara tam difficilia, quam rara sunt:* But all things excellent are as difficult as they are rare."

This is what Spinoza taught Goethe about true freedom. And this freedom—as exceptional as it is rare—this life's ideal, is what the erudite poet called nobility of spirit.

*   *   *

Throughout his life, Thomas Mann read Goethe. Toward the end of his life, he collected the essays he had written about the books that had become his friends, the masters who had become his contemporaries: Schopenhauer, Tolstoy, Fontane,

Lessing, Cervantes, Freud, and, above all, Goethe. The title
of this collection: *Nobility of Spirit: Sixteen Essays on the Problem
of Humanity.* It was 1945. Seldom would a title be this bitter.
Since then we have hardly heard of, or read about, nobility of
spirit. It became unseemly to talk about nobility of spirit, and
the ideal itself has been forgotten.

Nobility of Spirit

The Quest of Thomas Mann

Know then thyself, presume not God to scan;
The proper study of Mankind is Man.
—Alexander Pope, *An Essay on Man*

I

On September 1, 1939, at noon, when the radio announces that another war has broken out in Europe, the wife and a daughter of Thomas Mann consider whether to disturb him with this news. He is still writing, and the "sacred hours" during which he creates his work have not yet passed. Nothing bothers him more than to be disturbed, and the two women decide to let him be.

"Grab hold of time! Use it! Be mindful of every day, every hour! If you are not careful, time can slip away far too easily and quickly." This self-admonition in his journal is only one of the many illustrations of how Mann shares the conviction of his beloved mentor, Goethe, that *time* is our most cherished possession. Hence the value he attaches to his daily ritual. Get up at seven, have coffee and breakfast. At nine, retire to the silence of the study. There, seated at the mahogany desk that has traveled with him wherever he has lived, he works on his

daily *pensum*. Lunch at one, the newspaper and a walk. This is
followed by correspondence and studying. Tea at five, when he
receives friends. After dinner, music or further reading, and
before bedtime he writes in his journal to account for the way
he has spent his day.

In a short essay, "In Praise of Transience," published three
years before his death, Mann reveals the reasons for his respect
for time. This gift, he writes, must be sanctified, for it offers
the opportunity to develop our most essential talents. It is with
these talents that we, artists in particular, attempt to extract
the immortal from what is transient. Time is the space in
which to strive unremittingly for self-fulfillment, to grow into
the individuals we ought to be. This avowal is more than an
echo of Saint Augustine's call in his *Confessions* for everyone to
reflect on three things each day: who we are, what we know,
and what we want. It also expresses his belief in Goethe's answer to the question why his Faust, in spite of his great guilt,
can still be saved:

> He who strives with all his might,
> Can earn redemption still.

This man, who fears all his life that he might let one day go
by idly, who wrote in total concentration every morning—
even at the outbreak of a world war and his son's suicide—saw
his labors as an ethical commitment and hoped devoutly that
his diligence would justify his existence.

On June 6, 1950, Mann would be seventy-five, and in honor
of this festive occasion he was to lecture in various cities in the
United States and Europe. He puts the manuscript of *The Holy
Sinner* aside in February of that year—it is a novel about pen-
ance and the miracle of mercy—and thinks about the theme of

his lecture. Initially he plans to speak on the *pessimism* in Schopenhauer's view of humankind. Living as an exile in the United States since 1938, Mann is so disappointed with political developments after the war that the theme seems appropriate. But Katja, his wife, urges him to use the occasion of this birthday in the middle of a flawed century for a more "personal and general" lecture. The next day he writes in his journal: "The lecture ought to be personal, historical, autobiographical." Five days later: "Schopenhauer theme too academic. 'The Years of My Life' is preferable."

Early in his life Mann had already rejected the thought that he might be able to teach humanity something, not to mention the thought that his life might have pedagogical value. Wasn't he the solitary artist primarily concerned with the vicissitudes of his own life? When he received an honorary doctorate from the University of Bonn in 1919, he hastened to state in his letter of thanks that "I am neither a scholar nor a teacher, but rather a dreamer and skeptic, intent on saving and justifying his own life, not fancying himself able to teach something to improve people and win them over." But that was then. That was before he chose Goethe over Wagner as a model; before he continued life as a Nobel Laureate, fully aware of his representative role; before he came to America as an exile in 1938 and upon his arrival declared without a trace of irony: "Where I am, there is German culture." It wasn't without reason that he, the creator of three monumental European novels—*The Magic Mountain, Joseph and His Brothers, Doctor Faustus*—and an opponent of National Socialism from the early 1920s on, was known by his friends as "president of the spiritual republic." He realizes that the time has come to draw up his spiritual last will and testament: what humanity might learn from what he has learned. Katja is right once again. His autobiography could now be instructive. In the light of his life experience and his times, he would speak about the world and the questions of the only creature to whom it had been given to cultivate the field of time: the human being.

II

The old man could claim in his lecture, in all sincerity, that in his long and eventful life he had always been faithful to humanity, even when he still believed in the superiority of Germanness, criticized democracy, and denied the dangers of a separation between culture and politics. Those were the years of the First World War. By writing three articles in which he sang the praises of nationalism, he had joined the long line of artists who accompanied the German soldiers like bards. But the crisis in European culture that had exploded with this war made it virtually impossible for him to continue working undisturbed on what was originally intended to be a humorous novella: *The Magic Mountain*. Everything he had regarded as the spiritual foundation of his authorship had ceased to be self-evident. What is the essence of humankind? What values should society safeguard? What is the role of art in society? What ought to be the moral foundation of his own artistic existence?

All these questions are related, and as a young writer, Mann cannot justify practicing his artistic game without achieving new clarity about the moral pillars of his authorship. The need to subject his ideas on humankind, art, and society to a scrupulous analysis is reinforced and personalized in 1915, when his brother Heinrich rebuked him sharply and publicly because of his political stance. Already in doubt about what he actually thinks, and now deeply hurt—he does not speak to the brother closest to him for seven years—Thomas Mann decides to defend himself. Tense and embittered, he spends the war years working on *Reflections of an Unpolitical Man.*

When he starts writing these *Reflections,* he is convinced that the First World War is a conflict not about power but about spiritual ideas.

He believes that "German culture" is threatened. This heritage values personal growth through liberal education more than it values social commitment, and regards freedom as not so much political freedom as inner and spiritual freedom. Human happiness is a metaphysical and religious question, not a social problem; personal ethics are more important than social institutions.

He sees this heritage being threatened by the *Zivilisationsliteraten* with their "politicization of the spirit." The *Zivilisationsliteraten* (this neologism of Mann's is untranslatable) proclaim that all happiness is due to political ideology and social institutions. Thus human happiness is not a metaphysical or religious issue but a political problem. They believe in the perfect society and the perfect individual. It is this thought that most repells Mann, for it signifies the denial of what he considers the essence of existence: death; human limitations; the human being as the creature with questions to which no answers are forthcoming. This is why Mann loves *Parsifal,* for even if we are not quite as innocent as this fool, wouldn't we all do honor to our existence by being seekers, doubters? Human existence cannot be constructed; politics should not promise us happiness. Political thought is in no position to resolve life questions. As far as

Mann is concerned, only liberal education, ethics, religion, and art can guide us in this quest.

But, the writer determines, the "new times" propagated by the *Zivilisationsliteraten* will lead only to a further leveling out, vulgarization, and stultification. There will be no room for, not even interest in, inner growth, in the liberal education that, in Goethe's perspective, leads to respect—respect for the divine, for the earth, for our fellow human beings, and so for our own dignity.

Religion is argued away by complete rationality. Morality is replaced by a doctrine of virtue. But true morality allows for doubt, yes, even for sin, for an awareness of the demonic realm in which humanity can linger. All this knowledge and experience are more fruitful and lead more readily to humanness than does the new dogma of "Reason, Virtue, Happiness," which ignores everything human and will result in fanaticism and inhumanity.

In a politicized world Thomas Mann sees art suffering the same fate as morality. Art is made subordinate to ideology. All art must be socially engaged to the detriment of aestheticism. On the other hand, he is convinced that all great art does have moral value, but that no moral intentions, no virtuousness, may be required of art. He answers this early twentieth-century form of political correctness by quoting Goethe once again: "A good work of art can and will have moral consequences, but to require moral ends of the artist is to ruin his craft." Art is an irrational force that demonstrates, time and again, that the new doctrine of Reason, Virtue, Happiness does not provide humankind with the wisdom of life. Art has ethical value in Mann's opinion. But ethics is not the same as virtue, bourgeois decency, or any other politically desired morality. Art derives its ethical value exclusively from its aesthetic value, from its status as art—*l'art pour l'art*—from its independence, which is tied to its only purpose: to express beauty and truth. It is precisely because art does not ignore the demonic that it knows the depths of the human soul, that it can provide individuals with insights into themselves that they cannot acquire any other way. However, anyone who reduces art to a moral utility destroys art.

Will truth suffer a fate different from that of morality or art? No, for the "perfect individuals" who have no shortcomings—it is sufficient to conform to the ruling political ideology—think they can own the truth as they do virtue. Doubt is unnecessary, is in fact undesirable. But Thomas Mann has learned that no one can own truth and that, furthermore, humanity is better served by the quest for truth than by its alleged ownership.

However, he is as blind to social reality as he is sharp in seeing which ideas could safeguard or erode human dignity.

Thomas Mann never was a nationalist in the narrow sense of the word. He was too conscious that his republic was the world of ideas, of truth, beauty, and goodness, and that this world would never let itself be anchored to one specific place on earth. In his *Reflections,* he frequently refers to how he sees European culture, more than that which is typically German, as his spiritual world. At the same time, he makes the almost classical error of equating cultural conservatism (preserving a spiritual heritage) with political conservatism (maintaining an existing social order). Equating them means that the German Empire is better than the Western democracies. He concludes that politics distracts him from his artistic work and can be ignored as long as he is left in peace. The nineteenth-century world—of which he saw himself the progeny—should ideally continue to exist.

The most intelligent critique of this much-criticized book that is rarely read (and understood even less) is formulated later by Klaus Mann, his eldest son: "The unpolitical mind, when turning political, deemed it his foremost task to defend the somber grandeur of Germanic culture against the militant optimism of Western civilization. He confounded the reckless arrogance of Prussian imperialists with the splendors of Dürer, Bach, and Schopenhauer."

III

One of the Apocrypha, Ezra IV, offers the following story: While the Jews were in exile during the reign of Nebuchadnezzar, it happened one day that all Torah scrolls were destroyed in a fire. The prophet Ezra asks God what he should do. "The world is in darkness and its people without light. Your Law has been burned and no person now knows your rule." God gives Ezra the task of writing everything down again.

This is a well-known story in both the Jewish and the Christian traditions. Many monasteries have frescoes of Ezra writing down, once again, all that has happened since the beginning and all of the Law which God gave to the people.

In the twentieth century the Torah—that notable expression of what defines human dignity—is burned again. It is the poet Paul Celan who understands the *sensus moralis* of this historic event. People, he notes, should not speak anymore. Not only do their words "groan under the burden of a thousand years of false and distorted sincerity," they are fraught with the "ashes of burned-out meanings." Fire has destroyed the meaning of words: how can the individual know meaning, value, truth, when language no longer gives them expression?

The fire that blazes with the First World War, which is fanned even more in the Second World War and has still not been extinguished, did not come unexpectedly. A smoldering trace can be found both in German Romanticism, with its devotion to the irrational, and in the Enlightenment, where human reason was glorified as the measure of all things.

What was smoldering flares up in the revolution that takes place in the twentieth century: eternity is permanently dethroned. This, too, was expected—by Nietzsche and Dostoyevsky and by Baudelaire, who as early as 1863 comments in his "Painter of Modern Life" that "modernity is transitory, fleeting, contingent." This new sense of time is reinforced by technology. As a result, the Western world attributes superiority to everything that is new and fast and shows progress. History is excommunicated, as Osip Mandelstam concludes. Traditions do not count; eternity and transcendence are no longer recognized. The inexorable outcome of this new order is that meaning can no longer exist because it can no longer be known. At best, it is considered—for a moment, at one's own discretion. Measure, value, that which endures in the transient world—all disappear. They are replaced by nihilism, the cult of worthlessness. Truth is reduced to an empirical or mathematical reality and is no longer the ideal to which reality should aspire.

The "modern era" and the art it produces cannot be understood without an awareness of the loss of this eternity and the subsequent reactions.

At the mercy of the present and of mortality alike, a human being cannot be anything but rushed, harassed, adrift in a meaningless universe, haunted by lack of time. But people, as Socrates learns from Diotima, are in love with immortality, which renders them receptive to the "surrogates of God"— Nietzsche's words. The "Thousand-Year Empire" and the "Communist utopia" are invented explicitly as secular alternatives to the eternity that has been ousted. Today's Western society has the same aspirations as the Fascists and Communists. Not without reason do its most important pillars, the mass media and social-capitalist economy, proclaim the virtues of what is *new, fast, and progressive*—all on the level of consumer goods—and then offer us the *freedom* to be happy with our gadgets. We must feel eternally young, always see that which is new as superior, accept that limitations do not exist—and we'd better forget about death.

IV

The First World War confronts Thomas Mann with the question of whether his ideas about humankind, art, truth, and morality have lost their validity. His *Reflections of an Unpolitical Man* is the account of a painful but serious contemplation of these issues. In this connection, he also grows conscious of a far more basic question that has come to the fore, one that will captivate many others besides him: the question of time itself. What is the power of time? Can anything of lasting value, anything immortal, still exist in these new times? Is there a refuge for the dethroned eternity? And no artist can escape the question of whether his or her work could, or should, still have enduring value. Is it possible for something immortal to be expressed in a *contemporary* form?

Five days before he commits suicide, Vincent van Gogh sends a letter to his brother Theo, in which he mentions that

some of his paintings "maintain their calm even in the upheaval." If that can be a definition of great art—which it is, in
my opinion—then Joyce's *Ulysses,* Eliot's *Four Quartets,* and
Proust's *In Search of Lost Time,* but also Picasso's cubism, Schoen-
berg's twelve-tone music, and Heidegger's *Being and Time,* are
great works indeed. The challenge of the First World War is
accepted in them, and the twentieth-century paradox finds its
expression in them, too. Aware that any attempt to express
a new reality in an old language makes a lie of language, these
men manage to create a language that reveals modernity, the
supremacy of time, and a new perspective on human reality.
Theirs is a quest for a new dimension of eternity—which
Proust characteristically localizes in the "lost paradises" that
we can find again for just fleeting moments by chance and
"involuntary memory"—but at the same time, thanks to their
own language, these artists remove their creations from the
supremacy of time. The value of these works of art surpasses
oblivion and meaninglessness.

Thomas Mann is faced with the same challenge. Surrounded
by the distortion of life and the decay of values; seeing all
around him either a blind faith in unlimited progress and all
that is new or else a grim belief in what is old; blasted by the
ever-louder siren song of terrestrial eternity in the form of
totalitarianism, he also seeks an answer to the questions of his
era.

When he looks back on these years in "The Years of My
Life," he realizes that he has let go of the ideas in *Reflections of
an Unpolitical Man*—and did so almost immediately after its
publication in 1918. He did not let go of the values that he had
defended, however, but of his naive faith in conservative, nationalist politics as the guardian of his ideal world. In the end

he, too, arrived at the understanding that clinging to forms that have outlived themselves is not merely pointless but actually dangerous. To remain faithful to values is precisely why individuals must be open to a change in forms. Restoring historical forms that have lost their vitality is always a flight into obscurantism.

In January 1919 the German social-democratic newspaper *Vorwärts* asks Thomas Mann and his brother Heinrich, among other intellectuals, to provide a brief response to the question of what they expect of the new Germany. Although Mann in his *Reflections* placed the individual as a metaphysical being in opposition to the social perception of the *Zivilisationsliteraten,* his response now is surprising: "There is no doubt (and even those who in no way subscribe to Marxism as dogma and ideology cannot entertain any doubts in this matter) that the political future belongs to social ideas, in a national as well as an international connection." He does add, however, that if the social or socialist state should repudiate the civil spirit, then a society will inevitably lapse into the "dictatorship of the proletariat, of barbarism."

In *Reflections* the concept of *humanism* stands in opposition to the concept of *culture* and is the expression of his adversaries' superficial, optimistic, and democratic portrayal of humankind. In May 1921, however, he writes in his journal: "Discussions about the problem of German culture. Humanism not German, but indispensable."

This insight also grants him the courage to make peace with his brother when Heinrich falls ill. On January 31, 1922, he sends him flowers and encloses a card: "Those were difficult days that lie behind us, but now we have turned the corner and will go on in a better way—together, if you feel as I do."

In the summer of 1922, Walter Rathenau, the Jewish minister of foreign affairs in the Weimar Republic, is assassinated by
rightist extremists. Shocked and tormented by the question of
where this violence will lead, Mann decides to use the official
speech he is to give in honor of the sixtieth birthday of Gerhart
Hautpmann, the now almost forgotten but then famous writer,
to express public support for what he once opposed: the republic. The speech that he delivers on October 13, 1922, to a packed
hall in Berlin, the Beethoven Saal, is titled "On the German
Republic."

He tells his audience that war such as Tolstoy describes in
his great novel, war with a mythical-poetic element, no longer
exists. Today, war is an orgy of blood, destruction, and pure
evil. Anyone still looking for that larger-than-life kind of hero-
ism is a Don Quixote kind of obscurantist. Such obscurantism
is to be resisted, for beneath the mask of "fidelity to Germany"
lie only crudity and violence. Democracy and the republic
are incontrovertible facts. Anyone who is for "culture" must
now agree with peace, with the existence of a democratic
republic. Furthermore, one might wonder whether the former
German Empire hadn't, in fact, thwarted the attainment of
the German ideal, whether greater justice wouldn't be done
to the convictions of Goethe, Schiller, and Hölderlin in a
democracy.

Thomas Mann denies that he is betraying his own ideas
with these opinions. He explains that he wrote *Reflections of
an Unpolitical Man* as a defense of essential values. It is a conservative book, albeit on behalf of the future and not the past.
For the ideas in the book to remain fruitful, they must acquire
new forms and move along with the flow of life. And thus, he
has learned, a third element is needed to unite the secular and

the celestial, Enlightenment and Romanticism, reason and mysticism: humanism. This, according to Mann, is a classical word for "democracy."

Human existence may not be wholly spiritual or sensual, directed purely at either the metaphysical or the social. Whoever wants to pay homage to humankind cannot make do with one part only, Mann realizes. The entirety of existence must be known. And he warns that culture can degenerate into barbarism when sociopolitical developments are ignored. Anyone who would still deny that parliamentary democracy today safeguards human dignity and the survival of European culture is jointly responsible for the acts of extremists.

At that moment in German history, a sense of intellectual responsibility required Mann to express himself publicly on his country's social needs. He could not know how frequently he would have to fulfill that task again.

But one work of art can show us more than any number of political speeches can explain.

During those years after the war, the silent morning hours are devoted to the steadily growing manuscript of *The Magic Mountain.* That which before the war had been intended as a humorous novella now acquires a serious form: it is a new twentieth-century version of the myth of the Holy Grail. The supremacy of time and the quest for the eternal are not only the great issues of those years but also the theme of this myth. The community of the Grail—as the story of Parsifal, who is in quest of the Grail, tells us—is sick and at the mercy of mortality because the Grail, which gives eternal life, can no longer be revealed. European culture is suffering the same agony because eternity has been lost, its attributes of value and meaning included.

Monsalvat, the stronghold of the knights of the Grail, has thus become a sanatorium in Thomas Mann's version. Living high in the mountains with hardly any contact with the lowlands—everyday reality—the patients who reside there, and the reader with them, lose all sense of time and dwell in a kind of eternity.

A young man arrives, more or less haphazardly, in this timeless space. Initially he intends to spend no more than three weeks there, but he stays for seven years. During that period this Parsifal must try to understand something about life and, to this end, suffers through a number of pedagogical ordeals. He meets Settembrini and Naphta. The former represents the Enlightenment and believes in human goodness and in the omnipotence of human reason. He is equally and profoundly convinced that the fine arts will inspire people to good deeds. Naphta is his antagonist. He is a better judge of the darker side of humankind but expects well-being to come strictly from the totalitarian state, from absolute obedience, violence, and so forth. Opposing these "representatives of the European spirit" is the imposing Peter Peeperkorn, an uncomplicated, fat-bellied person, the symbol of life. Yet he is not a character to be emulated either. When illness prevents Peeperkorn from fully enjoying life, he lacks the mental strength to continue living and commits suicide.

What has our "innocent fool" learned about life after dwelling in the clouds for seven years? He discovers a pessimistic humanism that is familiar with tragedy and the limitations of human existence. Illness and death are part of life and cannot be denied; they provide us with a deeper understanding of the experiences of our existence than reason alone can offer. But he also learns that, for the sake of goodness and love, we may not allow illness and death, these dark powers, to rule our thoughts. He learns to admire the vitality of life but is also aware that life is always in need of a moral corrective, which is offered by the human spirit.

Mann later comments that the actual hero of his story is "the homo Dei, man himself with his religious question about himself, about his whence and whither, his essence and goal, his place in the universe, the secret of his existence, the eternally enigmatic obligation of humanity."

And what about the Grail that we are all looking for? The Grail, the time spent on the magic mountain teaches us, is not the cup of the Last Supper (which Indiana Jones was looking for more recently); it is, rather, a secret, an enigma. In fact, it is identical to the eternal secret of our own existence. Only when humans honor their eternal questions can they remain receptive to the values and meanings without which there is no human dignity. Being receptive will not bring eternal life on earth—earthly existence is and will always be transitory— but it will bring a survival of what ought to be eternal: the awareness of the transcendental values that encircle the enigma of human existence, like cherubs in the lost paradise.

"Time here becomes space"—so sing the knights of the Holy Grail in Wagner's opera when Parsifal enters the space in which the Grail lies hidden. There time becomes space, becomes eternity. Mann, too, lets us dwell in an eternity—the eternity of his story, the retelling of the myth, which is timeless because the quest for the Grail is timeless.

This eternity, this Grail—the eternal enigma of human existence—is his contemporary artistic answer to questions about time and eternity. It is also his timeless rejoinder both to the *Zivilisationsliteraten* who wish to deny this enigma and to the political and economic powers that in a variety of ways intend to lead people to their own grail: eternal power on earth.

Writing *Reflections* had been an ordeal. Writing *The Magic Mountain* was a quest for the Holy Grail. When, in his fiftieth year, Mann writes "finis operis" underneath his novel's last sentence, he has gained the insight that denying this secret or accepting any surrogates is bound to lead to the destruction of the one thing to which he wants to be faithful: humanity.

V

In the spring of 1934, Thomas Mann has what will be his final encounter with the man who has been like a father to him, who through the self-confidence he gave the young writer— "Why not write a novel? Just don't make it too long."—allowed his artistry to flourish: Sammi Fischer, the Jewish publisher in Berlin who was responsible for the publication of all Mann's books, including his first novel, *Buddenbrooks* (which was nevertheless voluminous).

When they see each other in Zurich in 1934, Fischer's health is already in decline. He is old, deaf, frequently confused, and disheartened by the terror the Nazis are perpetrating in his beloved Berlin.

Less than six months later Mann is obliged to write an "In Memoriam." In it he recalls a moment from that meeting, when the aged Fischer offered an opinion of a common acquaintance:

"Not a European," he said, shaking his head.

"Not a European, Mr. Fischer? Why not?"

"He has no understanding of the great humanistic ideas."

Mann continues: "I cannot say how shaken I was. This was a voice from an almost bygone era, a generation that was greater and better than the one now taking the reins."

The great humanistic ideas: that is European culture. That is the tradition Mann consciously accepted when writing *The Magic Mountain*. At the same time that this monument of European humanism is published, however, the frightening question arises: Is it a culture that will endure, or will it prove to be merely an episode in history?

In Germany—the same Germany in which so many great minds helped to shape European culture—a previously unknown hatred of this culture manifests itself with escalating vigor. When the Nazis obtain their first great electoral victory in September 1930, Mann again raises his voice in public. On familiar territory—the Beethoven Saal in Berlin, where in 1922 he justified his choice for democracy—he speaks about his country's political developments. He outlines how, in a climate in which technology, sports, movie stars, and the power of large numbers are idolized, room is made for "politics in the grotesque style, with Salvation Army posturing, mass fits, showground peals of bells, hallelujahs, and dervish-like repetitions of monotonous catchwords, until everyone is foaming at the mouth, fanaticism turns into a principle of deliverance, enthusiasm into epileptic ecstasy. Politics becomes an opiate of the masses in the Third Reich, or proletarian eschatology, and reason veils her face."

Culture is being destroyed to make space for a new cult. *Bildung*, the moral and spiritual formation of the human being, is no longer allowed to exist. The people want to be submerged in a collective high, freed from individual responsibility. Nazism is a revolting form of religion. It is an orgiastic worship of nature, hostile to humanity. The ultimate goal of this belief is obvious to Thomas Mann: the obliteration of truth. For totalitarianism can exist only by the grace of the lie and violence.

In "The Years of My Life," Mann declares that his disgust with any form of totalitarianism is based on the fact that such ideologies always venerate the lie. He declares that as a writer, as someone who depicts what is human, he can only devote himself to the truth.

But what is truth? For Mann truth is not an empirical or mathematical concept. Truth is not reality. On the contrary, truth is measure and value, the ideal to which every human must aspire. That is why he names a journal *Measure and Value* when he helps to establish it in 1937 to give voice to the "other Germany." In his editorial introduction he states that it is high time to give back to certain words their rightful meaning. Truth, for example, is not a relative, subjective concept to be dealt with at one's own discretion. Truth is the absolute standard by which the level of human dignity is to be measured.

This less than contemporary view of Mann's is the logical result of his vision of humankind. Because we are human, he says, we are more than our physical selves. This *more* should be part of the definition of being human. One side of man is animal, but the other side links him to a spiritual realm. "Consciousness teaches him to draw distinctions. As the Lord God says in Genesis, he is 'like one of us'; he knows what good and evil are, he possesses the absolute. The absolute is given to him in the ideas of truth, freedom, and justice, and with these ideas comes the dream of redemption, planted in him by the shortcomings of the natural world, the dream of sheer perfection."

At the time he was writing *The Magic Mountain,* he describes the essence of humankind as the "eternal enigma that man is to himself." This enigma consists of two elements. On the one hand, there is human nature, that which is mortal and which all too often is the source of the tragedy of life. It is the element that he emphasizes in his debate with the *Zivilisationsliteraten,* who believe in the idea of the perfect human being. On the other hand, thanks to the spiritual abilities of human beings, each person knows the absolute, knows the immortal values that everyone must try to realize, as Mann never tires of saying.

Goethe continues to be the star witness. "All laws and conventional rules can be traced back to a single thing: the truth," observed the learned poet from Weimar. What he taught his student about the essence of freedom is no less important: "Freedom consists not in refusing to acknowledge anything above us, but in revering something that is above us."

The truth sets us free because it has power over us; it gives us instructions, not the other way around. However, this absolute, inaccessible truth that our consciences can know but never possess, cannot, by definition, be curtailed by any transient form of truth. Therefore, no mortal can ever own the truth. Orthodoxy—whether theist or atheist—becomes fundamentalism when this essential truth is not respected. The ever-changing world constantly demands new forms for revealing the truth. Another word for these forms is "culture." Annihilation of culture signifies annihilation of the truth. And annihilating the truth is nothing less than depriving the individual of dignity.

VI

If humanity, truth, and eternity are big words—bigger, in any event, than what we are accustomed to these days—then

let us justify artistic existence as lifelong faithfulness to
language.

Every poet knows that the gift of the gods is not fire but
language. "Man dwells poetically on this earth," Hölderlin
wrote. Language is the essence of being human. We can think,
thanks to language, for thought exists only by the grace of
words. Our experiences and emotions are molded by language.
It is language that allows us to name and know the world. We
ourselves are known by language, through prayer, confession,
poetry. Language gives us a world that reaches beyond the
reality of the moment, to a past (there was . . .) and a future
(there shall be . . .). It is through language that eternity has
a space and that the dead continue to speak: "Defunctus adhuc
loquitur" (Hebrews 11:4). Thanks to language, there is meaning,
there is truth.

Language cannot tolerate lies. A lie renders words mute,
seizes their soul. It is not by chance that language was the
greatest concern of such writers as Aleksander Wat, Anna
Akhmatova, Primo Levi, and Victor Klemperer. Each of them
was forced to experience the cult of the lie. Like Paul Celan,
they knew that wherever the meaning of words is destroyed
by fire, truth and humankind burn with the words.

Thomas Mann saw it as his responsibility to take language
back from the liars. That is why he continued to write, why he
retold an old story. He had no need to be original. Hadn't his
mentor confided to his editor and memoirist Eckermann that
recounting the truth in a morally confused world is in itself a
virtue?

While the Teutons in Mann's homeland celebrate their anti-
humanism, consider themselves to be the chosen people, and
see Hitler as their savior, Mann opposes their new religion with

a different myth, religion, and God. From 1927 to 1942 he continues to write "this invention of God, this beautiful story of Joseph and his brothers." It is the myth that narrates how human beings discover dignity by following in the footsteps of Abraham. For it was the idea of the man from Ur that whom he serves is of the greatest importance to humankind. And he decides: "I, Abram, and humankind within me, may serve only what is highest." That was the beginning. At first Abram thought that the most important thing was the earth, but it needs rain from heaven. Then he assumed that it was the sun that he sought, but the sun sets, as do the moon and the stars. It was through the realization that God surpasses everything else that he discovered God.

God is the world's space, but the world is not His space. It is this unimaginable, purely spiritual and moral God that Abram discovers, and the two of them make a Covenant.

Myths are the earliest signs of the human spirit. In them the most profound human experiences became language and could be told. A myth is timeless because the experiences recounted are as old as humankind. All meaningful life is mythical life, which is to say that we all follow in footsteps. Yet human beings are responsible for choosing the steps in which they tread.

Joseph, Jacob's son and the hero of this tale, is conscious of the fact that he—and we with him—must follow in the footsteps of Abraham, Isaac, and his father in order to acquire dignity.

Does Joseph merely repeat what has come before? Yes and no. He learns that the secret of the myth he chooses is not just a repetition of the past but also a step forward, a matter of changing, being open to what is new. The myth's "once upon a time" is the past, but it is the future as well. "Eternal" means "always," but it also means "that which is yet to come." Joseph's religiosity is thus shaped by "*attentiveness* and *obedience;* attentiveness to the inner changes of the world, the mutation in the aspects of truth and right; obedience which loses no time in adjusting life and reality to these changes, this mutation, and thus in doing justice to the spirit. To live in sin is to live against the spirit, to cling to the antiquated, the obsolete, and to continue to live in it, due to inattentiveness and disobedience."

Joseph, so his story teaches us, has to let himself be guided by "concern with God."

When Thomas Mann finishes the narration of this tale in January 1943, Europe is under the domination of those who do not wish to engage with the "concern with God." They are following the path of a different myth.

After this novel about the beginning of the history of salvation, the discovery of God and human dignity, the narrator realizes that he has to write one more book, which for him could be his last. It is that other myth: a timeless story about pride, a pact with the devil, and the end of time.

On Sunday, May 23, 1943, Mann begins his *Doctor Faustus: The Life of the German Composer Adrian Leverkühn as Told by a Friend.* In this life story he recounts the vicissitudes of Germany, the crisis of an era, the crisis in art. It is the bitter tale of intellectual arrogance and moral blindness, the proximity of aestheticism and barbarism as the result of the cult of art, the delusion that humankind can save itself.

Adrian Leverkühn is to compose two great works, the first one of which, in 1919, is the *Apocalipsis cum figures.* In this opus he holds a mirror of revelation up to mankind so that it can see what is soon to come: the end, the judgment, the doom that is on its way. A choir sings one of Jeremiah's Lamentations:

Wherefore doth a living man complain,
A man for the punishment of his sins?
Let us search and try our ways,
And turn again to the Lord!

. . . .

We, we have transgressed
And have rebelled:
Thou has not pardoned.
Thou hast covered with anger, and persecuted us;
Thou hast slain, thou hast not pitied.

. . . .

Thou hast made us the offscouring
And refuse in the midst of the people.

Serenus Zeitblom, the friend who is also the story's narrator, tells us that this work stands in contrast to a Romantic work of redemption; it is characterized by its theologically negative and merciless character. With this work the composer succeeds in revealing the deepest secret of human beings in musical form: our ambiguity, the identity of the animal part of us with our most purely sublime part.

The second composition—after which this man of genius will come to rest in a mental darkness from which he will never escape—is the symphonic cantata *Lamentation of Dr. Faustus.* This work is emphatically written as the counterpart to Beethoven's Ninth Symphony. The paean to all that is good, joyful, and hopeful is revoked by Leverkühn with his lament, a terrifying accusation of humankind and God.

Zeitblom points out that the work is marked by a constant reversal. This Faust rejects any thought of salvation as itself a temptation—not only out of formal loyalty to his pact with the

devil and because it is "too late" but also because he despises
the positive optimism of the world for which he is to be saved,
the lie of its godliness. His rejection of the thought of salvation
is a proudly despairing "No!" to false and flabby bourgeois piety. But Zeitblom, who knows his friend's work better than any
other person does, divulges a completely different reversal of
meaning at the end of the cantata, where the last agony of
doubt is expressed, sounding like God's lament for the lost
state of his world: the Creator's sorrowful "I did not will this."
At this point the narrator wonders: "Is it here, in this tone
poem that permits no consolation, reconciliation, or trans-
figuration, that the religious paradox can perhaps be found,
that out of the profoundest irredeemable despair, if only
as the softest of questions, hope may germinate? This would
be hope beyond hopelessness, the transcendence of despair—
not its betrayal, but the miracle that goes beyond faith."

Thomas Mann never concealed the fact that *Doctor Faustus*
was his most personal work: a confession. In the early days of
his exile in the United States he declared without reticence:
"Where I am, there is German culture." Throughout his life he
saw himself as a child of the nineteenth century and German
Romanticism. He was the embodiment of Germanness and
was, more than anyone, profoundly convinced that Nazism was
not primarily a political phenomenon but a cultural one—
rooted in his German culture. In order that people would here-
after know how the greatest annihilation can be ignited in a
great culture, he could do nothing other than plumb the depths
of his own soul and recount the story of his life and times.

VII

The years of farewell have arrived when Thomas Mann delivers "The Years of My Life," his speech at the University of Chicago on April 22, 1950, before an audience of fifteen hundred people.

His final years are dictated by disappointment. His fidelity to humanity finally led him to understand that what this world needs above all else, a social order that would safeguard human dignity, can come into being only through a new humanism—a religious humanism that respects the impenetrable human secret, does not deny the human tragedy or humans' demonic depths; that acknowledges the truth that can be known only by our consciences as the absolute standard to which we must aspire; that incorporates the entirety of our existence and does not ignore the political reality.

Right after the Second World War, in his lecture "Nietzsche's Philosophy in the Light of Our Experience," he warns that no conference, technical measure, or judicial institution, nor even a world government, can possibly bring the new society one step closer if it is not preceded by a different spiritual climate, a new receptivity to the *nobility of spirit*.

But the only thing that happens is a further poisoning of the political climate. There is a Cold War, and a new politicization and national hysteria, this time in America with McCarthyism. The FBI has opened a file on Mann and two of his children, Klaus and Erika, that is more than a thousand pages long. The most notable charge: premature anti-Fascism—that is to say, resistance to Fascism before America declared war on Germany in late 1941. This, according to the FBI, could prove only one thing: sympathy with Communism.

Mann doesn't hide his disappointment with the cynicism of the Western democracies. For the sake of their economic interests, they first put up with the rise of Fascism and Nazism as the best weapon against Bolshevism, thereby sacrificing the Czech people in 1938. Now myopia and economic interests are once again the rule. In the West, they refer to "democracy" as the justification for a policy, but no one has any inkling of what the essence of a democracy might be. In *The Coming Victory of Democracy* (1938) Mann had pointed out that aristocracy and democracy weren't really opposites. Indeed, if aristocracy truly means "leadership by the finest and the best" then it is precisely what he understands democracy to be. True democracy can't do without an aristocratic bent—it must have a nobility, though not by birth but of spirit. "In a democracy that does not respect intellectual life and is not guided by it, demagogy has free rein, and the level of the national life is lowered to that of the ignorant and uncultivated. But this cannot happen if the principle of education is allowed to dominate and if the tendencies prevail to raise the lower classes to an appreciation of culture and to accept the leadership of the better elements."

Under these circumstances he lets himself be drawn into giving speeches and performances that make it look as if he might accept Russian totalitarianism; he even visits the part of Germany occupied by the Soviet Union. To prevent an unwelcome riot, the Library of Congress in Washington, D.C.—the place where "The Years of My Life" was initially supposed to have been delivered—tells its "Consultant in Germanic Literature" that he had better not appear that year. Thomas Mann never appears there again. He bids good-bye to America. After the death of Roosevelt, whom he so admired, it can no longer be his country.

He returns to Europe—to Switzerland, for Germany can no longer be his country either. It is there that he wants to say farewell to his earthly existence, conscious of the fact that with him the world will say farewell to bourgeois humanism and its era. The Europe of Sammi Fischer, the culture of the great humanistic ideas, has passed into oblivion. In his darkest moments he anticipates for the West the coming of a "long night utterly devoid of education and memory."

He was at the height of his fame, yet despair over the significance of his existence had never been greater. He had built a life on Goethe's moral principle of renunciation. He had practiced this form of asceticism, which had protected him from surrendering to all kinds of temptations and had helped him to use his time constructively. He was still at his large mahogany desk at exactly nine o'clock every morning to write during the quiet morning hours. But the hours dragged on when the paper remained blank. What could justify his existence under these circumstances?

"I have chosen the melancholy that hopes, strives, and searches over the melancholy that despairs in sorrow and paralysis," Vincent van Gogh wrote in one of his letters to his brother. It is this melancholy that Mann finds in the work of Anton Chekhov, a man, and an oeuvre, to whom in his final year of life he devotes one of his most beautiful essays.

What he recognizes in the life and work of the young short story writer are his own work ethic, human skepticism, irony, and the notion that the capacity to change oneself is the most important moral duty.

Mann was deeply affected by Chekhov's *A Dreary Story,* in which a despairing young woman asks an old and very learned man what she should do with her life. Despite all his experience and knowledge, the professor has nothing more to say than: "Really, Katja, I don't know."

Mann's reading of Chekhov's stories confirmed his deep-seated belief that "truth's salvation" cannot be provided by a human being, nor can art save humanity. At best, art, beauty, and stories can free the human soul from fear and hatred and thereby guide the individual further along on the journey through life. Art cannot be power, but it can offer consolation—not in the sense that it tells us life is good, for that would be a lie, but in the sense that it shares our questions and deepest emotions.

Thomas Mann hoped that his novels, the most precious fruit of his hours of contemplation, would offer this consolation to his readers. Then his time would have been well spent, and his existence would be justified. Then perhaps mercy would be his.

Untimely Conversations on Timely Questions

> There is too much betrayal, there is too much
> a general sphere of intellectual disgrace.
> —Stephen Spender, *World within a World*

I

Some conversations are unforgettable.

In a magnificent house near Piraeus, the harbor of Athens, a small group of affluent young men has gathered to wait for the celebrations later that evening in honor of Artemis, goddess of the hunt. Summer is approaching, the afternoon is warm, and the hours threaten to crawl along. Near his home, the host happens to run into a friend who is legendary for his gifts in the art of debate. Gently but firmly the host invites him to join the group, for what could better dispel lethargy and idleness than a good conversation? He is an odd person, this particular friend. His clothes and lack of footwear demonstrate that he is either not very well off or not interested in outward display. He is small, middle-aged, and solidly built. The friendly eyes in his bearded face betray a good nature and a sharp wit. When Cephalus, the host's elderly father, realizes that Socrates is in his home, he greets the unexpected but welcome guest warmly. Socrates inquires courteously after the health of the old man, who is approaching the winter of his time on earth. Cephalus answers that he has no reason to complain and explains that dealing with old age is all a matter of character. If you yourself are cooperative and friendly, you will be treated the same way, and then old age is hardly a problem. Socrates agrees, but wonders at the same time whether it is perhaps not the great wealth of his aged friend rather than his character that has made it easier for him to accept growing old. According to Cephalus, having or not having money does makes a difference, but character is of much greater importance. Socrates' graciousness has to surrender to his unremitting curiosity about the actual meaning of statements made, and he asks the old man, "What is the most significant thing you owe to your vast fortune?" The old man responds that for fear of what might await in Hades, anyone who senses the approach of death is bound to examine his past in order to determine whether his has been a just life, whether he ever treated anyone unjustly. "My wealth," the old man says, "has made it easier for me to live a just life, for he who is rich has no need to be guilty of deceit or lying, nor does he need to leave any debts behind."

But is justice the same as "speaking the truth" and "returning what one has been given"? Is wealth a condition for the ability to be just? What is justice? What is the meaning of justice? Why should a person seek to be just? Is the life of the just actually happier than the life of the unjust? Suddenly many questions emerge that relate to the subject dearest to Socrates: "For it is no ordinary matter we are discussing, but the right way to live."

They have the whole afternoon—a good time for a good conversation.

Glaucon, one of Plato's older brothers, is able to illustrate the problem by telling the following story. Once upon a time a shepherd found a golden ring that made its bearer invisible. The shepherd could now enter the palace, seduce the queen, kill the king, and assume power. What if, Glaucon asks, there are two such rings, and a just person and an unjust person are each wearing one? Why continue to be just when you have the power to seize whatever you desire, can copulate with any woman you wish, can kill, can, in short, take any liberty at all, like a god among mortals? For Glaucon this is proof positive that it isn't out of their own free will that people are just, and that anyone who dares to be honest will deem injustice to be far more profitable than justice.

To Socrates, however, the height of injustice is to appear just without being so. The person who is truly just doesn't merely want to appear good but wants *to be* good. Neither reward nor reputation is of any interest to the just person. Socrates will have to convince his friends that justice is good, that injustice is always evil, and that in the end, therefore, the happiest individual is the one who is just.

To plumb the essence of justice Socrates suggests that they examine the meaning of the word within a larger context: the state. On the basis of those findings it should be easier to determine the characteristics of the just individual. In the subsequent discussion they come to the conclusion that the best state is a society in which human dignity is guaranteed for all citizens. Wisdom, bravery, and moderation will reign. And justice will be present in that all citizens will have that to which they are entitled and which is appropriate for them to have.

Having what is appropriate, the just person will be a model of human dignity. The just person will be wise, will love the truth, and will not know infidelity, adultery, parental neglect, or disregard of the gods. Because reason restrains the unreasonable part of the just person's soul, the just person will be well versed in moderation and courage. Justice cannot exist without knowledge of what is good, as the subsequent conversation clarifies. The highest virtue provides the just person with the knowledge that is most crucial: knowledge of what is best and the ability to distinguish between good and evil. The yearning for justice produces a restless quest for what is good and for an existence that is in harmony with one's own soul and one's fellows.

What, then, can injustice possibly have to offer? Licentiousness, cowardice, ignorance. Is the unjust individual happy? Socrates responds with a rhetorical question: "Is there anyone who, on the basis of this line of reasoning, can profit by acquiring gold unjustly when, because of this acquisition, the result is tantamount to subjugating his noblest self to the most inferior part of himself?" No, the happiest life is the life of the just.

Thereupon Socrates comes to a logical and yet surprising conclusion. If all people are to do what they are most skillful at, then the country's leadership—which entails responsibility for the creation and maintenance of the laws assuring beauty, justice, and goodness—should be entrusted to those who are most experienced in doing what is best and who know the distinction between good and evil. And with a solemn voice Socrates declaims: "Unless either philosophers become kings in our states or those whom we now call our kings and rulers take to the pursuit of philosophy seriously and adequately, and there is a conjunction of these two things, political power and

philosophical intelligence, there can be no cessation of troubles,
dear Glaucon, for our states, nor I fancy, for the human race
either."

*   *   *

Evening has not yet fallen. The conversation between
Socrates and his friends continues. But his last comment—
that the only perfect state can be the one that is ruled by philosophers and intellectuals—has already generated the memory
of a different, no less unforgettable conversation. Once again
it is afternoon, a Sunday afternoon, to be exact, and once again
it is summer, but this time we need not be concerned with
the lethargy of Mediterranean heat. Summer afternoons in the
Swiss mountains are pleasant. This particular afternoon we
find a group of four men in a fairly spacious room of a small
house in Davos Dorf. The host is a thin, rather unattractive,
but well-dressed Jesuit, though of Jewish descent, who used to
teach classical languages. Suffering from tuberculosis, he was
forced to seek the pure high-mountain air. Occasionally he still
teaches at the local secondary school, but apart from that, his
monastic order supports him. The youngest in the group is a
blond man in his early twenties, a recently graduated civil engineer. He came to Davos for three weeks to visit his slightly
older cousin, a lieutenant in the Prussian army, who is also
present. However, during his visit he, too, has been diagnosed
with a light case of tuberculosis, and everyone considers it ad-
visable that he not return to the lowlands for now but remain
in the Berghof Sanatorium.

The cousins originally intended merely to pay a courtesy call
on the teacher, but they have only just entered when the third
guest appears: an elegant gentleman with a black mustache and
a weakness for checked pants. He is an Italian and a man of

letters with a deep passion for the classical humanistic tradition. Pedagogy, too, is a beloved vocation, and he sees the young engineer as someone he will be able to initiate into the wisdom of his tradition. The Jesuit—actually a housemate; the humanist lives on the attic floor—is, because of his convictions, his opponent. There is polite respect between the two intellectuals, but the differences of opinion are so vast that there can be no question of mutual understanding.

A fourteenth-century pietà owned by the host—a wooden statue that causes the young engineer to wonder how something could simultaneously be so ugly and so beautiful—leads to a discussion about the primacy of the spirit versus the primacy of nature where beauty is concerned. The humanist suggests that anything spiritual that does not reflect human beauty and dignity cannot be truly honorable. Furthermore, it is not without reason that this statue was created during the horrors of the Inquisition, when the postulated well-being of the human soul was considered more important than individual freedom.

The Jesuit retorts that the true degradation of the individual did not begin until the Renaissance, the development of natural sciences, and the focus on "objective knowledge" and "objective truth," which have practically nothing to say about the spiritual welfare of humanity. It would have been better if the Catholic Church had retained absolute power and if humanity, under the church's leadership, had been preoccupied with the only knowledge that matters: the knowledge of God.

"But that is absolutism of the state," the humanist objects. "That is precisely how all doors were opened wide to every form of criminality and how human dignity, individual justice, and democracy were ousted from society."

His opponent is not impressed. "Your ideals," he said, "the ideals of liberalism, individualism, and humanistic citizenship, came to an end long ago—they are dead or, at best, lie twitching in their death throes, and those who were to have been finished off have got their foot in the door again. You call yourself, if I am not mistaken, a revolutionary. But you are badly mistaken if you think that future revolutions will end in freedom. After five hundred years, the principle of freedom has outlived its usefulness. A pedagogic method that regards itself as a daughter of the Enlightenment and employs educational methods based on criticism, on the liberation and nursing of the ego, on the breaking down of ordained living patterns—such a pedagogy may still achieve moments of rhetorical success, but for those who know and understand, it is, beyond all doubt, sublimely backward. All institutions dedicated to genuine education have always known that there can be only one central truth in pedagogy, and that is absolute authority and an iron-clad bond—discipline and sacrifice, renunciation of the ego, and coercion of the personality. It is ultimately a cruel misunderstanding of youth to believe it will find its heart's desire in freedom. The mystery and precept of our age is not liberation and development of the ego. What our age needs, what it demands, what it will create for itself, is—*terror*."

Silence falls. After a little while the otherwise so eloquent humanist, still shaken by what he has just heard, asks, almost crestfallen: "And who will be the agents of this terror?"

First the Catholic expounds the good reason why traditionally the church, as the instrument to guide humanity back to its original heavenly state, had priority over the secular state. He upbraids the pale man of letters. "You try to correct the nation-state with a little liberal individualism, and call it democracy; but your fundamental relationship to the state remains completely untouched. You are apparently not disturbed by the fact that money is its soul. Or would you contest that? Antiquity was capitalist because it idolized the state. The Christian Middle Ages clearly saw that the secular state was inherently capitalist. 'Money will become your emperor'—that is a prophecy from the eleventh century. Do you deny that it has literally come true, making life itself a veritable hell? It is the political ideology of your bourgeois class, the freedom of your capitalist democracy, that has ruined the world. Since the days of Gregory the Great, the founder of the City of God on earth, the Church has seen it as her task to bring mankind back under divine rule. His papal claim to temporal authority was not made for its own sake; proxy dictatorship was, rather, a means, a path, to a redemptive goal, a transitional phase from the heathen state to the kingdom of heaven. Your state believes in the freedom of trade, capitalism. The Church fathers called 'mine' and 'yours' pernicious words, described private property as usurpation and thievery. They repudiated private ownership, since, according to the divine law of nature, the earth is the common property of all mankind, and therefore its fruits are likewise intended for the common use of all. They were humane enough, anti-commercial enough, to call economic activity a danger to the salvation of the soul, that is, to humanity. They hated money and finance and called capitalist wealth fuel for the fires of hell. They considered the peasant and the craftsman honorable people, but not the merchant or the industrialist. They wanted goods to be produced on the basis of need and loathed the idea of mass production. Well, then—after having been buried for centuries, all these economic principles and standards have been resurrected in the modern movement of communism. The correspondence is perfect, down to the meaning of international labor's claim of dominion over international marketeering and speculation. In the modern confrontation with bourgeois capitalist rot, the world's proletariat embodies the humanity and criteria of the City of God. The proletariat has taken up Gregory the Great's task, his godly zeal burns within it, and its hands can no more refrain from shedding blood than could his. Its work is terror, that the world may be saved and the ultimate goal of redemption be achieved: the children of God living in a world without classes or laws."

This conversation continued, there on the magic mountain, where the banalities of the lowlands seemed so distant. And yet the small Jesuit Communist intellectual, who relentlessly prophesied the era of terror but was equally convinced of the historic necessity of the proletarian dictatorship, better understood the signs of the times than did his much more likable humanist challenger. "The Golden Age of Certainty" of the bourgeois capitalist society was still around, but the world's downfall was waiting to happen. In Russia the Bolshevik Revolution began after the First World War broke out, and it brought not freedom but terror, just as the intellectual guardian of the human soul had predicted. In the person of Lenin the Socratic wish was fulfilled: an intellectual became king.

* * *

Yet another conversation is etched in the memory of European history. Although this one takes place in Munich, not all that far from the mountain on which the previous discussants were present, and only six years later, the European world has radically changed. The First World War has come to an end, as has the German Empire. In Russia the dictatorship of the proletariat is a fact. What will Europe's future be?

In Schwabing, Munich's neighborhood of artists and intellectuals, leading minds gather regularly for their "gentlemen's philosophical discussion night" at the home of Sixtus Kridwiss, the well-known graphic artist and book illustrator. And so they meet again on the spring evening of 1919, where we find the erudite Dr. Chaim Breisacher, a scholar; Dr. Egon Unruhe, a philosophical paleontologist; Professor Georg Vogel, a man of letters; and the art historian and Dürer specialist, Professor Holzschurer. An affluent manufacturer and a few members of the upper nobility—friendly young men but none too bright— have kept their evening open for this gathering as well. Furthermore, the celebrated poet Daniel Zur Höhe is there to read from his *Proclamations,* one of which ends with the exclamation "Soldiers . . . I entrust to you the plundering—*of the world!*" "Marvelous," "Beautiful, very beautiful," they say when the poet takes his place at the table again.

After the lofty art of poetry they return to the topic of conversation: perspectives on current social reality. There is a lively sense that the war disrupted and destroyed what had seemed to be life's fixed values. It is an emotion deeply felt and, according to them, objectively confirmed in the monstrous loss of self-worth that each individual has suffered through the events of the war, in the disregard with which life strides right over every single person nowadays, and in a general indifference to each man's suffering and perishing that has found its way into people's hearts. This disregard, this indifference toward the fate of the individual, might well seem to have been sired by the recent four-year bloody circus, but, as they argue, one ought not to be misled—for here, as in many other regards, the war had only completed, clarified, and forged as a common drastic experience something that had long been developing and establishing itself as the basis of a new sense of life.

The democratic republic and its freedoms are not accepted for a single moment as a serious framework for the new situation these gentlemen have in mind, but are unanimously shrugged off as self-evidently ephemeral, as predestined to meaninglessness in the present situation—indeed, as a bad joke.

Reflections on Violence, a book by Georges Sorel published seven years before the war, plays an important role in the conversations of this culturally critical avant-garde. His unrelenting prediction of war and anarchy, his characterization of Europe as the soil of armed cataclysms, his theory that the nations of this continent have always been able to unite around only one idea, that of engaging in war—all that furnished grounds for *Reflections* to be called the book of the age. They are enthusiastic about Sorel's conclusion that henceforth popular myths, or, better, myths trimmed for the masses, would be the vehicle of political action; fables, chimeras, phantasms, that needed to have nothing whatsoever to do with truth, reason, or science in order to be productive nonetheless, would determine life and history and thereby prove themselves dynamic realities. The book's most important thesis is that violence will be the triumphant counterpart of truth. This thesis makes it possible to understand that truth's fate is closely related to that of the individual, is, indeed, identical with it— and that fate is devaluation. The book opens a sardonic rift between truth and power; truth and life; truth and community. Its implicit message is that community deserves far greater precedence, that truth's goal is community, and that whoever wishes to be part of the community must be prepared to

jettison major portions of truth and science, to make the
sacrificium intellectus.

The intellectuals are animatedly discussing the arrival of an
old-new, revolutionary, atavistic world in which values linked
to the idea of the individual, such as truth, freedom, justice,
and reason, are sapped of every strength and cast aside, or,
wrenched free of pale theory, have at least taken on a very different meaning from that given them over the past centuries
and now, relativized and red-blooded, are made applicable at
the currently much higher level of violence and authority, and
to the dictatorship of belief. Humanity will be transferred,
along with all these new ideas, back into the theocratic situation of the Middle Ages; but according to these well-read men,
this process will be no more reactionary than the path around
a sphere can be termed regressive. Regress and progress, the
old and the new, past and present—all become one, and the
political right coalesces more and more with the left. Consequently, this company is unanimous in its opinion that all humane pampering and emasculation, which has been the work
of the bourgeois epoch, must make place for mankind's instinc-
tively getting into shape for hard and dark times, that would
scoff at humanity for an age of great wars and sweeping revolution, presumably leading far back beyond the Christian civilization of the Middle Ages and restoring instead the Dark Ages
that preceded its birth and had followed the collapse of the culture of antiquity. Civilization, Enlightenment, humanity. They
are gone. It is the age of a new barbarism.

Such was the diagnosis in Munich of Europe's future on that
early spring evening of 1919. What is striking is that these intellectuals, who themselves represented the European cultural
traditions, made the diagnosis of the future without much con-

cern. On the contrary, they considered barbarism the return-and-advance to the era preceding European civilization rather interesting, even positive, merely because the recognition thereof was a sufficient accomplishment, and entertaining as well. It was entertaining because these leading minds tended to sympathize with the destruction of those life values that had all too long been considered sacrosanct.

When Thomas Mann, who had already chronicled the loss of European civilization in *The Magic Mountain* (1924), with a shudder recorded this particular discussion verbatim for coming generations in his *Doctor Faustus,* the vision of his city's cultural elite had become a reality. The foundations of a civilization that was more than two thousand years old were being destroyed; violence and power were victorious over truth and freedom.

"Unless either philosophers become kings in our states or those whom we now call our kings and rulers take to the pursuit of philosophy seriously and adequately, . . . there can be no cessation of troubles . . . for our states, nor I fancy, for the human race either." Is this true, Socrates?

*   *   *

On September 11, 2001, nineteen men hijacked four airplanes in the United States. One plane crashed—probably owing to a struggle between the passengers and the hijackers. Another plane demolished a wing of the Pentagon. The other two planes flew straight into the towers of the World Trade Center. More than three thousand people lost their lives, including all the planes' passengers, people in the towers when they collapsed, and more than three hundred firefighters and police.

Political leaders and most of Western society see the attack as an assault on Western civilization. A sizable group of prominent and leftist intellectuals do not share this view. "The homeless, the powerless, the terrorized, the minorities are using terror to strike back"—thus the Dutch journalist Van Houcke. Dario Fo, the Italian Nobel Laureate in literature comments: "The great speculators wallow in an economy that every year kills tens of millions of people with poverty, so what are 20,000 dead in New York? Regardless of who carried out the massacre, this violence is the legitimate daughter of the culture of violence, hunger, and inhumane exploitation." Susan Sontag wonders: "Where is the acknowledgment that this was not a 'cowardly' attack on 'civilization' or 'liberty' or 'humanity' or 'the free world' but an attack on the world's self-proclaimed superpower, undertaken as a consequence of specific American alliances and actions?" Norman Mailer says to an enraptured audience in Amsterdam: "Everything wrong with America led to the point where the country built a Tower of Babel, which consequently had to be destroyed. America is a country without roots, without culture, dominated by television and commerce. The country is dulled, dumber; money has made every value secondary, we have become obsessed with it. The attack should be seen as a criticism, and the true test of a great country is that it can tolerate criticism."

These perspectives on September 11—emblematic and representative of a mindset shared by many renowned intellectuals in Europe and the United States—add up to the following: there is no question of an attack on Western civilization. On the contrary, these acts of terror are the logical response to a society that has sold its soul to money: commerce, capitalism, globalization, a policy of "interests." The September 11 deaths of three thousand people in the country that is the incarnation of all these evils are the inevitable result of the *lack* of civilization.

The discussions between the Communist Jesuit and the humanist man of letters in Davos Dorf before the First World War ended in a duel. Not only were there fundamental disagreements but the subject of the continuing conflict itself was fundamental: What is civilization? What image, what ideal of human dignity, is to be its connective tissue? What values, what qualities of life that provide this ideal with its life blood, are to be respected and protected? These are fundamental questions because their answer is decisive for the moral standard by which our actions are measured; for the distinction between good and evil; for the answer to the Socratic questions: What is the good society? What is the right way to live?

That Thomas Mann, in his chronicles about the fortunes of his homeland, could not think about the discussions of his fellow citizens without horror is because once again the civilization of the West was being discussed—and rejected. Nazism came to power in Germany.

Was the September 11 attack directed at Western civilization, or was it the consequence of a lack of civilization in the West (the United States in particular)? The question is important because the answer affects the future of Western society: the Western ideal of civilization. One thing we certainly already know is this: if the discrepancy between politics and people on the one hand and the intellectual elite on the other —"guardians of civilization," as Socrates called them—is so huge as to be irreconcilable, then the ideal of civilization, whatever it may be, is in deep trouble.

*   *   *

In Western cultural history "civilization" is a relatively young notion. The word itself, as defined by the French thinker Condorcet, does not become a standard term until the second half of the eighteenth century. It means a society that needs *no violence* to introduce political change. No one has absolute power, because the powers are separated, and political, intellectual, religious, and artistic freedoms are guaranteed by a constitution and by institutions that are to safeguard the democratic freedoms.

In *Observations Concerning the Distinction of Ranks in Society* (1773), the relatively unknown Scotsman John Millar probably uses the term "civilization" for the first time; he defines it as "the gentility of mores which is the natural consequence of abundance and security." There is no civilization without prosperity and security. The break with the closed feudal system, the rise of the bourgeoisie, cities, trade, a commercial economy, and democratic freedoms are the most important stimuli for both cultural flowering and the development of different forms of civilization. It is obvious, however, that both factors— prosperity and security—are necessary to the creation and the survival of a civilization, but they never guarantee its actual existence. Prosperity and security are the conditions for civilization to exist, not the values that shape its essence. If security is the exclusive aim of a society, that society will create a police state that lacks the freedoms by which a civilization is nourished. And a society that elevates material prosperity to an absolute value will not have a civilization either, and will perish as a result of its decadence.

Measured by its own ideal of civilization, Western society is in a profound crisis. It is impossible for anyone who is attached to this ideal of civilization not to be critical of today's society. Nevertheless, one basic standard of civilization still holds true: *no violence* is needed to bring about political change. Trade unions, environmentalists, human rights activists, and many more of the socially committed can attest to the achievement of far-reaching social changes without using violence—although change is always excruciatingly slow to come and requires endless effort and great power of conviction. The possibility of nonviolent change exists because the powers are divided and democratic freedoms and human rights are guaranteed. After the dark episode of totalitarian violence—from which Europe was notably saved by the United States—this is one of the few historical lessons that have penetrated the very fibers of Western society. Anyone who still uses violence to accomplish political ends excludes himself or herself from dialogue and is uncivilized.

The terrorist attack on September 11, 2001, was not the work of "the homeless, the powerless, the terrorized, the minorities." The opposite is true. The action cost half a million dollars and was mostly the work of well-educated, affluent men whose ideology was identical to the medieval theocratic ideal for which the German Fascists of 1919 yearned. The worldview of the Taliban—the sect to which the terrorists were closely connected—is totalitarian and fascistic, this time in the form of Islam. Whoever listens to them will again hear the voice of the Jewish-Catholic Communist in Davos. No freedom whatsoever will be tolerated, whether political, intellectual, artistic, religious, or sexual. The main rule is absolute obedience to the omnipotent religious leaders, who, in accordance with their ideology, are to purify the world from all that can possibly corrupt the souls of true believers and thereby threaten their earthly utopia. This "corruption" begins with the existence of "unbelievers," that is to say, all those who do not subscribe to the true dogma—more specifically, that part of humanity that adheres to political, intellectual, artistic, religious, and sexual freedom. The symbol of military might, the Pentagon, and the symbol of prosperity, the World Trade Center, where people from many countries, from all across the globe, worked, became the target of violence precisely *because* both buildings symbolized the conditions of security and prosperity that allow Westerned civilization, with its values and freedoms, to continue to exist.

The evil mind behind the attacks has made it clear through frequent messages that there should be no mistake about the ultimate goal: the annihilation of "unbelievers"—their civilization, their values, and their freedoms. That goal will not be reached until his totalitarian ideology is victorious. In that respect, September 11 was merely the beginning of a holy war. It is precisely in this one goal, and the unimaginable hatred that it represents, that the much-sought-after cause, reason, and breeding ground for September 11 are found.

*   *   *

In the totalitarian thinking of the Taliban, women have no rights, homosexuals are executed, and art—including sculptures of the Buddha thousands of years old—is destroyed; anyone who thinks differently from what the religious authorities prescribe will not be tolerated.

It is remarkable that in a world where so much is reported publicly, this violent medieval theocracy could be installed without the Western intellectual elite ever making a single attempt to put a stop to its barbarism.

It is remarkable that this same critical community has no compassion whatsoever for the victims of September 11, all those men and women whose sole remains consisted of uncollectible dust in a vast ruin. Their names are not mentioned by the critical elite, not even known; they have actually been deprived of them as their lives are reduced to an abstraction. The attack was not on them, say these critics, but on capitalism, globalization, Americanism.

It is remarkable that reductionism, in every respect, determines the analyses and evaluations of so many of the 9/11 pundits.

Anti-Americanism is undeniable. In terms of approach, there is no difference, for instance, between anti-Semitism, anti-Islamism, and anti-Americanism. In each case a plurality is reduced to a single one-dimensional image, to which the "anti" judgmentally attributes all sorts of characteristics. Subsequently, that caricature is held up as the only true image of Judaism, Islam, or the United States. Let's confine ourselves to the last. For the anti-American, "America" is always capitalism, commercialism, mass consumption, kitsch, the bogus, hamburgers, no traditions, television, superficiality, militarism, imperialism, and so on. Every time that anti-Americans are confronted with just one of these phenomena they see "America." Therefore "America" is always bad, for nothing positive fits this barren image. Not so very long ago, a similar reductionist myopia saw everything by and for the proletariat as good and everything by and for the bourgeoisie as evil; now the "poor" are always victims and the "rich" are always criminals. Because "America" is rich and can therefore never be a victim, everything that happens to America or Americans is always their "own fault." This is an outstanding example of the intellectual approach of ideologists who reduce reality to a political vision in which only "left" and "right" continue to exist. The notions of good and evil and all morality are politicized and poured into the ideological mold. Everything on the "left" is right; everything on the "right" is wrong. This is why it is not so remarkable that the anti-American mind attributes a moral legitimacy to the cynical murder of three thousand innocent people. Obviously, this murderous assault was a crime, *but . . .* there is capitalism, globalization, imperialism, militarism, own fault, not without blame. Thus the victims are to blame, the attackers are not so blameworthy, and the evil of murder is not so terrible. "America" is always evil, and therefore any attack on America must always be good; the mass murder is therefore an act that we-don't-excuse-but-we-do-understand, a justification that fits within the criticism of a society that falls short of the professed ideal of civilization. This manner of reasoning is not new. The salon Fascists in Munich and the intellectual apostles of the Communist utopia, basing their thinking sometimes on a social critique of society that in principle was not unjust, always thought they needed to justify the deeds of the Men of Action: Hitler, Stalin, and their ilk. Raymond Aron correctly points out that these intellectuals are always merciless toward the shortcomings of democracy but enormously tolerant of the greatest crimes when these fit within their ideological perspective.

Something else that is not new is the fascination with, sometimes even the idolization of, deeds and violence committed by those who represent the spiritual world. It is no coincidence that we already find a vivid illustration of this worship in Goethe's *Faust:*

> "In the beginning was the Word": why, now
> I'm stuck already! I must change that; how?
> Is then "the word" so great and high a thing?
> There is some other rendering,
> Which with the spirit's guidance I must find.

We read: "In the beginning was the Mind."
Before you write the first phrase, think again;
Good sense eludes the overhasty pen.
Does "mind" set worlds on their creative course?
It means: "In the beginning was the Force."
So it should be—but as I write this too,
Some instinct warns me that it will not do.
The spirit speaks! I see how it must read,
And boldly write: "In the beginning was the Deed!"

The media caused a great uproar by calling the attack "cowardly." Typical was the comment of Mailer to his audience in Amsterdam: "We have completely lost our respect for language. A democracy cannot function without respect for the accuracy and intensity of language. Take a competent bureaucrat like Colin Powell—how can he speak of a cowardly attack? That is a grandiose misuse of the language. It may have been a monstrous act, demonic, base, but how can you call these terrorists cowardly? . . . Americans can't bear to say that such an act takes courage and that those people might even be admired perhaps, for that could be misinterpreted. The crucial point is that we in America are convinced that they were blind, insane fanatics who didn't know what they were doing. But what if those perpetrators were to be right and we were to be wrong?" So spoke the self-professed guardian of the language.

A few weeks later the evil genius who planned the 9/11 attacks had the floor again. This time he said that most of the hijackers had *not* known what was to happen. Not until they entered the planes were they given instructions to take them over, and they still did not realize they were about to meet a certain death. And as the man recounts this he chuckles cheerfully at his own cleverness. Although the men who piloted the planes did know the whole plan ahead of time, they could count on the highest reward—the finest place in paradise—and what could earth possibly have to offer by comparison?

The question remains: How courageous can you really be when you do not even know that you are collaborating in your own death? How courageous are you when you have nothing to lose because divine paradise awaits you? And why should someone be *admired* when it is unbridled hatred that drives him to destroy as many lives as possible? How "accurate" is the word "admire" in this case? Moreover, according to some language purists, the firefighters who ran into the inferno in New York out of a sense of duty in a final attempt to save human life may not be called "heroes." They were "naive," we are told.

How do you cut reality into pieces? You cut it in three. You throw away the truth because you already have your own ideology. You push goodness aside because political dogma has its own morality. What remains then is "pure beauty" and "sublime action," which the amoral aesthete extravagantly admires.

Language exists to name reality, and in that respect language has an almost sacred function: without language we can never know what is true, good, or beautiful. Karl Kraus, Victor Klemperer, Aleksander Wat, Thomas Mann—many poets and writers have pointed out that when language is assaulted, the lie will eradicate the truth of its soul. But naming the truth begins with allowing reality to exist in its entirety, not with reducing it to one's own image and semblance.

The poet knows that not everything can be named. The philosopher knows that not everything can be explained. And anyone with any life experience knows this, too. Hatred and evil can never be wholly explained, just as love and goodness cannot. These phenomena cannot be reduced to "reason" and "cause." It is precisely the fact that they cannot be rationalized— and thereby be made manageable and solvable—that gives them such power. Insanity, hatred, and jealousy are irrational, blind forces. Someone possessed by them goes blind and— once again—reduces reality. That is the secret of every enemy stereotype. Reduce a person to an *Untermensch,* and you will be able to kill that person without scruples; reduce a person who thinks differently to an "unbeliever," and the fundamentalist no longer needs to respect him or her; reduce friends, mothers, fathers, children, loved ones, workers in the World Trade Center to "capitalism and globalization," and you need not shed any tears over their deaths.

"O! Matter and impertinency mix'd, / Reason in madness," Edgar whispers, horrified, when he hears the mad King Lear ranting and raving at Gloucester, his father, whose eyes have been put out by Lear's vicious daughters. Not everything a madman shrieks has to be nonsense. Every now and then some truth may be contained in what he mutters. Still, "reason in madness" does not mean that the madness can be rationalized and made into reason. It is not by chance that the better part of the "explanations" and "breeding-ground theories"—if they aren't utter nonsense to begin with—explain little or nothing. What an examination of such "explanations" clarifies is the desire to project all criticism of the West (the United States) onto the "deed" and, consequently, not to have to judge that which is *inexplicable:* the existence of evil. In the meantime, the brain behind the attack, along with his circle, is thrilled about the "annihilation of thousands of unbelievers . . . many more than we could have hoped for." Dostoyevsky would have called these men "demons." That is the only correct characterization.

The journalist Van Houcke writes in his public journal:
"The more clearly the artists, thinkers, writers speak out,
the more conspicuous is the lack of insight among politicians."
The opposite is true. There are too many intellectuals who
legitimize what should never be legitimized: mass murder.
Intellectuals who subordinate the distinction between good
and evil to the dogmas of their political ideology. Intellectuals who make great verbal noise but offer no insight into
reality and merely reduce it to their nemesis, a nemesis
steeped in resentment. This is the betrayal of the intellectuals,
but the history of the twentieth century shows that that,
too, is not new, alas.

II

There is another unforgettable conversation, unforgettable
because of its great importance. In contrast to the three memorable conversations already mentioned, this one, which took
place off the main stage of European history, has never been
as widely known as it deserves to be.

On the evening of October 29, 1946, four men gather in a
house on the edge of Paris near the Bois de Boulogne. It is a
large house, decorated with an impressive collection of paintings and statues. André Malraux, the host, who knows all
four of the visitors well, lets them in. An author, politician,
and public intellectual, he is not only wealthy and famous but
also—as a man who can always count on having the ear of
General de Gaulle—at the center of power in postwar France.
His visitors include the Hungarian intellectual Arthur Koestler,
who became well known during the war years for his novel
Darkness at Noon (1940), a bitter indictment of the lies and vio-

lence of Stalinism, and Koestler's friend, Manès Sperber, the German Jewish writer and psychologist. Jean-Paul Sartre, who in contrast to Koestler is sympathetic to the Soviet Union and firmly anti-American, is there as well. The fourth and youngest one in the group is the writer and journalist Albert Camus.

The reason for the meeting is their shared concern over the current political situation and its implications for the devastated European civilization. The war is over. The United States is victorious and has the atomic bomb. Stalinist Russia is victorious and almost has the atomic bomb. The four are convinced that intellectuals should take the initiative where the two superpowers are concerned. Human rights now have to be defended *everywhere*. In France itself the League for Human Rights is too closely linked to the French Communist Party, which in turn is spoonfed by Moscow. The topic of conversation is the question of whether it might not be better to establish a new, more independent human rights organization with an international reach.

Koestler begins. "It is vital for everyone that a minimal code of political morals is formulated. And we, we intellectuals, must stop offering all sorts of specious arguments that presumably are useful to the case in point and yet will never be so. Recently an interviewer asked me whether I hated Russia. I told him that I hate the Stalinist regime as much as I hated the Hitler regime, and for the very same reasons. But if you have to admit *that* after so many years of struggling for the ideals of Communism, then there is no hope! What is left? What means of action do we still have?"

Malraux, who had been a Communist himself, defines his political position. In principle he is still interested in supporting something, but he cannot, and will not, have anything to do with organizations or individuals that still believe that truth is embodied by the "proletariat." He puffs his cigarette and signals a servant to fill his wineglass. "Why would the greatest historical value lie with the proletariat?" he concludes, as if that's all there is to it.

Sartre, who is ill at ease, takes the comment personally. He has never been particularly fond of Malraux—whom he considers a narcissistic bourgeois capitalist wearing a leftist mask. He should not have come. He wants nothing to do with Malraux and, to the surprise of his friends, now suddenly declares himself against the plan. "I've given it some thought. Your organization will end up turning against the French Communists, and I cannot and will not abandon those who protect the interests of the oppressed. I can't turn my moral values against the U.S.S.R. exclusively, although it is true that the deportation of several million people is worse than the lynching of one black man. However, the lynching of a black man is the result of a situation that has existed for a century or more and represents the misfortune of just as many millions of black people as the millions of people deported from Chechnya."

Koestler is annoyed. Had he not just observed that the first thing intellectuals should do before taking any political action is distance themselves from their own sophisms for the greater glory of the Big Idea? He comments curtly: "It needs to be said that we, as writers, betray history when we don't press charges where charges must be pressed. In the eyes of those who come after us, we will be condemned for a conspiracy of silence."

Malraux has to smile. Sartre says nothing and looks at Camus. He is not surprised that Koestler repudiates the proletariat, but he is curious about the young Camus. Camus knows what Sartre expects of him, but his sympathies lie

with Koestler. The latter knows, as does he, what poverty is—
something the philosopher does not, even though he constantly
preaches about the proletariat—and Koestler has distanced
himself definitively from communism, as he himself has done
as well. Camus is convinced that if intellectuals are not able to
take truth itself as the only guideline for thinking and acting,
then their political morality, too, is bankrupt: "Don't you think
that we are all responsible for the lack in values? And if we,
who come from Nietzschean thought, nihilism, or historical
materialism, were to openly declare that we were wrong, that
moral values do exist, and that from now on we will do all
that is necessary to establish and clarify them, don't you think
that this will offer a beginning of some hope?"

Koestler nods approvingly, Malraux looks at his cigarette
thinking that this is of no use to him politically, and Sartre
decides that he will never again set foot in this house and will
explain it all in further detail to Camus later. The conversation
is brief; everything has been said. It is time to go. At home,
Camus makes brief notes about the discussion in his notebook.

We cannot forget this conversation—however brief and
unpleasant it was—because it expresses what the essence of
civilization is, how it can be lost, what the task of intellectuals
is, and what their betrayal means.

*   *   *

Civilization. There can be no civilization without the realization that human beings have a double nature. They have a
physical, earthly existence but are distinguished from other
animals by *also* having a spiritual being and by knowing the
world of ideas. They know about truth, goodness, and beauty,
are familiar with freedom and justice, love and charity. The
basis of every form of civilization is the concept that humans

derive their dignity and true identity not from what they
are—flesh and blood—but from what they should be: the
embodiment of these immortal life-affirming qualities, these
values that encapsulate the finest aspect of human existence,
the image of human dignity. "It is material weight that gives
its value to gold and moral weight which gives value to man,"
as Baltasar Gracián says in his masterly *The Oracle, a Manual
of the Art of Discretion* (1646).

These values are universal because they are the same for all
people, and timeless because they are of all time. Culture is the
knowledge and shaping of these intangible spiritual qualities,
collected in the cultural heritage. Only those works that are
themselves timeless are significant; they continue to speak to
us from generation to generation because they are the only
works that express a timeless reality, an idea. It is precisely this
requirement, this characteristic of timelessness, that renders
all of culture and all spiritual values defenseless. Culture has to
be defenseless, purposeless, and disinterested. Therein lies the
secret of its timeless significance. A cathedral, a poem, a sculp-
ture, a myth, a string quartet, a song may not be functional
or useful at its core. All these works have something to tell us,
not the other way around. The only correct attitude toward
timelessness is a receptive, answerable, and disinterested one.
Only then, when we listen, look, experience it that way, will
the creations of the human spirit—albeit "without words"—
"speak of their contemplation and the eternal mystery" (J. H.
Leopold's phrase). A cultivated person is therefore the direct
opposite of all those (utilitarians, materialists, ideologues) who
reduce everything to the question: Of what use is it to me?
What can I do with it? No one can ever know any truth or
value without the open-mindedness and answerability neces-

sary to reach beyond appearances. It is not without reason that Kant speaks of the need for "disinterested pleasure" and that Gracián notes in *Oracle* that "unprejudiced thinking has always been the breeding ground of wisdom and a source of joy for righteous people."

What is civilization? In his brief but brilliant book, Gracián summarizes the idea as follows: "Man is born a barbarian; he is saved from being a beast by acquiring culture. Culture, therefore, makes the man, and the greater his culture the greater the individual." Let us return for a moment to the warm afternoon in Piraeus, where Socrates and his friends are discussing the meaning of justice. Glaucon initiated the conversation with his story about the ring that could make people invisible and thereby omnipotent—thereby turning them into beasts. This is the same barbarian that Gracián describes. You are a barbarian if you do not possess, and apply, the only knowledge that matters to human dignity: you must practice the virtues and be guided by the spiritual values that make a harmonious existence with your fellows possible. In Goethe's consummate words: "Civilization is a permanent exercise in respect. Respect for the divine, the earth, for our fellow man and so for our own dignity." This is the same refinement of which Gracián speaks, the elevation of the human being above what he also is: a blind force, a barbarian.

Admittedly, this human ideal is an aristocratic one, although it concerns not the nobility of blood but the nobility of spirit, which any individual can acquire, and it is the timeless ideal of civilization. "Nobility is present wherever virtue exists, but virtue is not always present in the nobility," as Dante wrote.

Guarding this ideal is the task that Socrates assigned to the intellectuals. What is the right way to live? is the moral question with which civilization begins, and intellectuals are those privileged to derive their eminent position ("distingué") from the primary task: to distinguish ("distinction"). For the sake of the survival of civilization, intellectuals have the duty to safeguard and pass on their knowledge of what is best and most valuable. They must be educated in the knowledge of what is true, make the distinction between what is and what is not of value, what is good and what is evil. And it is precisely because the spiritual values of existence are universal and timeless that they must be transcendent absolute values. Still, not a single mortal can ever own them, which is why none of those who know what is best will ever claim to possess complete truth, and why discussion, as in the Talmud, never ends.

These are——or should we say these *were?*——the parameters of the ideal state and the ideal human being that Socrates sought when he wanted to find the meaning of the value of justice.

*   *   *

In a small village near a lake surrounded by mountains, a solitary person lives in a simple room. There are a bed, a small table with a washbasin, and a larger table between a bare bench and a wooden chair. When a migraine doesn't force him to stay in bed during the day, he takes long walks in the woods and along the lakes. In his solitude Nietzsche writes by the light of an oil lamp at night: notes, letters. On July 2, 1885, he writes to a distant friend: "The current age is so vastly superficial that I am sometimes ashamed to have said so much in public which at no time, even in much more valuable and deeper times, should have been made public. This century of 'freedom of the press and for impudence' has spoiled taste. But I do it in the example of Dante and Spinoza, who were better prepared for the fact of loneliness. Of course, their manner of thinking was, in contrast to mine, more suited to enduring loneliness; and in the end, everyone who still has 'God' for company will not know the loneliness that I experience." He stares through the small window but because of the wall of darkness sees only his own reflection. He places the pen in the inkpot and adds one more sentence: "My life now consists in the *wish* that all things might be *otherwise* than I take them to be, and that somebody might make *my* 'truths' appear implausible to me."

Yes, so it was. Being alone doesn't necessarily mean being lonely. Nor does having distant friends—there are always those friends who never leave you and with whom you can still have a meaningful conversation. I have books. Dante, Spinoza, Goethe. But even they wouldn't understand me. True friendship, male friendship, wouldn't be possible, not even with them. I do understand them, but they do not understand me. The same goes for this era. I have come too soon. Loneliness. I have no choice. What was it Luther said when he had to answer for himself? "Here I stand. I cannot do otherwise." Ah, Luther. He certainly could write. Just compare his language with the drab prose of today's theologians. Scribblers! Cultivated philistines! Luther undeniably loved drama and thrived on attention and fame. Ah, to be pope himself, power. Whoever seeks public fame wants only that. "Bene vixit qui bene latuit." *Tristia* by Ovid. Students were obliged to translate this: "Whoever lived beyond the limelight lived well." They didn't get it. Publicity! The newspaper! That is their Valhalla. What was it I told them then? "You've replaced your morning prayer with reading newspapers." They liked that. Didn't get that either, apparently. And these are the educated. I even gave lectures about liberal education. Explained then, too, that no person would strive for

Bildung if it were understood how incredibly small the number of the truly educated was and actually could be. People can fool themselves in myriad ways. The gratifying word *Bildung* has been robbed of all of its meaning and is no more than a finely painted but empty shell. Utility has been declared the most important goal in life—or, to be more exact, earning as much money as possible has. And I, who assumed the noble task of training the youthful elite, my work was downgraded to training *marketable* people. Everything had to be marketable, up to date, adapted, current, and, above all, not different, not difficult, not weighty, common—common most of all. Only then could they most easily earn money, only then would everyone be happy. Not too difficult, Professor. Please! For any *Bildung* that would make one *lonely,* that would not be concerned with making money and profit, that would take time, that was the kind of liberal education *I* would offer, was "higher egoism," was "indecent cultural Epicureanism." This would be funny if it weren't so tragic. Universities. Professor at twenty-five. A good thing I stopped teaching seven years later. Migraine. Well, that diabolical pain has been good for something, at least. The entire university is corrupt. Marketable people. That's where they are. That's how they are trained. To conform. The new definition of what is best. To adapt—to money and the public, obviously. Intellectuals will never save this world. They don't really need to. The world will go under anyway. All they do is hasten the process. They can't write anymore either. Let them improve their style. That will also improve their thinking. What now? I live like Ovid in my self-imposed exile. I write books that no one reads. I've discovered the truth that no one understands. I'm forty and feel old. I feel as if I'll never grow old. My loneliness lies in *my* truth. I've never allowed them to corrupt me. Have always been faithful to thought. Pascal. Crazy, of course, with his self-torture. But brilliant and real. Sham—everything in today's Christianity is a sham. Virtuous-ness is hypocritical, and dutiful obedience is called piety. I have respect for Pascal. "Thus all our dignity consists of thinking." Right. Perfectly true. I had no other choice but to keep think-ing. Be faithful to thought. Dare to recognize reality. Socrates. It started with him. Dante, Spinoza, Pascal, Goethe! Even though the genius from Weimar was a heathen, his profound sympathy with the ethics of the Gospels makes him part of the group. The lonely and their God. They are lonely, but I am even more so. My time will come. Goethe. More European than German. Therefore a great man. "Our whole feat consists in giving up our existence in order to exist." Brilliantly phrased, but incorrect, dear Goethe. There is nothing other than this daily, physical existence. That's it. Beyond this, above this, any-where out there, there is nothing. *Nothing!* That is the key to my truth. Nihilism. There are no immortal, universal, timeless values because there is no timelessness, no transcendence. It is empty. A great void. No truth, no beauty, no goodness. *I* exist. That is all. *My* truth is all there is, *my* beauty, *my* morality, *my* justice. To each his own. Take your choice. Nihilism. It's right at the door, but no one understands the consequences yet. Ladies and Gentlemen! The Truth does not exist. Never did. But they made you believe in it because without your religion, without morality, without your metaphysical chains, you and all your prissy respectability, you will behave like *beasts.* Giving speeches makes no difference. They don't listen and they under-stand even less. The great secret of nihilism: nothing makes any difference. Only non-sense! For anything that could provide human existence with meaning, all the values that people abide by because they are universal and eternal, have vanished into the great void together with eternity. There is no world of ideas. There is only nature. Be true to your body, your instincts, your desires, your chaos. Anything is allowed, for nothing is superior to us. Boundless freedom without any meaning. That is life. Socrates' ideal of human dignity was an idée fixe. The only ideas that will survive. Would always survive. For what will these ignorant intelligentsia do when the highest values are lost? When the meaning of existence is lost? New little deities will appear. Each club with its own little deity, its own idée fixe. A deity for the nationalists, a deity for the socialists, a deity for the capitalists, a deity for the rationalists. Each with its own little deity. They will hate the Jews. Next to the little deity, a little scapegoat. It's peculiar how humans can't do without the absolute. My human would be different. An *Übermensch* who needs no absolute. He is strong enough to accept the nonsense. He doesn't conquer others, only himself. I have liberated myself. They have not. They can't handle freedom. For them freedom becomes a curse. Socrates already knew this. That warm afternoon in Piraeus: I actually read that famous conversation with my students in Greek. The good society, the philosopher-king, and then the discussion about the collapse of the ideal state. In the oligarchy where the rich are in power, the people, the poor, rise up, and a democracy is established. Now everyone is free, all people can say what they want, and arrange their lives as they deem fit. Coercion no longer exists, and because coercion isn't allowed, the first thing to disappear will be education. With the disappearance of *Bildung,* virtues, too, will vanish. And then there is this marvelous passage: "The soul, purified of virtues, will bring in the new masters, Insolence, Anarchy, Prodigality, and Shamelessness, resplendent,

with a great attendant choir and crowned with garlands, and
in celebration of all the praise they euphemistically denominate
insolence 'good breeding,' license 'liberty,' prodigality 'magnifi-
cence' and shamelessness 'manly spirit.'" Plato knew how to
write. On the following page the tirade against freedom—
hungry for freedom, the democratic state won't know how to
be moderate: "And do you note that the sum total of all these
items when footed up is that they render the souls of the citizens so sensitive that they chafe at the slightest suggestion of
servitude and will not endure it? For you are aware that they
finally pay no heed even to the laws, written or unwritten, so
that forsooth they may have no master anywhere over them."
I haven't left anything out, fortunately. The only way to get to
know a text is through translation. And now, tired of freedom
after the era of freedom, one would presumably welcome dictatorship. So I do agree with that Greek on something. In the
end, people experience freedom as a burden. Better to obey.
True. No, Socrates wasn't stupid. *First proposition:* Without nobility of spirit a democracy will fail because of its own freedom. *Demonstration:* See the present time. Liberal education
disappears, virtues disappear, eminence disappears, the art of
distinction disappears, silence disappears, the contemplative
life disappears, the spirit disappears, morality disappears, *thou
shalt* disappears. *Second proposition:* The above is inevitable.
Demonstration: Socrates' own yearning for truth. Only the truth
would be valid. Well, then, faith in the absolute is a lie. This
has been researched and proven. Logic, Ladies and Gentlemen.
Please, just a bit of logic. There is no transcendence! There
is no eternity! There is no immortality. You haven't encountered it, I haven't encountered it, no one has encountered it.
Therefore there are no immortal values. Therefore there is no

transcendental ideal image of the human being to which everyone must aspire. You may again be loyal to the earth and to
nature. Everything is allowed. You are doomed to freedom.
Nothing is true; everything is allowed. Am I making myself
understood? Have I been understood? It is inevitable, Socrates,
it is inevitable: the dehumanization of nature and then the
naturalization of humans. After freedom, terror. I know it.
And art. Oh, God. Yes, art, too, will disappear. *The Divine
Comedy,* Raphael's paintings, Michelangelo's frescoes—
they won't exist. Art's greatest masterpieces have exalted
humanity's religious and philosophical errors, expressed faith
in the absolute truth of these ideas. As this faith ends, art
won't flourish any longer, and the meaning of these works
will disappear. And music? Your music? You've been dead two
years now. Two or seven, since we didn't exchange a single
word during your last five years of life. Our friendship was
dead. You were dead. I was dead. The soul doesn't exist, but
if I ever had a soul, it died at that moment. Because of you.
You are the only one I ever loved. Nobody else. And won't
again. Dying once for love is enough. Our friendship was true
friendship. Male friendship. I understood you, you understood
me. How often were we not together? How many plans did
we not make? How much did I not do for you? My colleagues
began to hate *me* because I kept singing *your* praises. But I
always remained faithful to you. As faithful as Elisabeth to
Tannhäuser, Senta to Hollander, Elsa to Lohengrin, Brünhilde
to Wotan, Kurnewal to Tristan. And you? Why did you have
to betray me? You crept back toward Christianity and em-
braced that damned Church of Rome again. You disavowed
my truth. You shouldn't have done that. Not you. I could have
forgiven you anything else. Your gushing over these stupid

people, your stupid anti-Semitism, your narcissism, your
hunger for luxury and fame. Anything, but not your asserting
the very lies that *I* exposed. You were never strong enough
to be a free spirit. The world is too important to you. It is
precisely because of your love of money, lust for fame, anti-
Semitism, and nationalism that you betrayed me. That you
couldn't be faithful. You couldn't take criticism, and your
father-in-law's religiosity pleased you. I loved you. I was faithful
to you. Why did I have to become your worst foe? Why did
I have to kill off my love for you? For you and your divine art.
You wanted to be God's ventriloquist. Savior! And I? What
was it you told my doctor? That I'd gone *mad* from too much
masturbation. That I was a pederast. Projection, my love.
Projection. No matter. It's over. It's all over. It's cold here.
My life is cold. I feel dead. It's all dead. There is no absolute
truth. There is no love. And that is fine. The only thing that
could have made my truths implausible is your love. Your
love would have been my eternity. Because of your love
I would have imagined everything that is dead to me to be
alive. Do you see it, friends? Don't you see it? Headache.
I must get to bed.

* * *

Nietzsche's era—"once the old God has abdicated, I shall
rule the world from now on"—the era of nihilism, manifested
itself far earlier than he had dared suspect. Fourteen years
after his death the First World War broke out. Then Europe
was in the grip of Fascism, Communism, and Nazism.
Another world war broke out. An orgy of violence triumphed
over truth, goodness, and beauty. The ideal of civilization
was despised. Tens of millions of people cheered, admired,
and furthered the violence. Tens of millions of lives were

annihilated. Nihilism always and inevitably ends in violence and annihilation.

Nihilism always begins—Nietzsche's lucid analysis leaves no room for any misunderstanding here—with robbing human existence of the possibility of elevating the self above its animal nature. This robbery both of eternity and of the spirit endows humanity with the nobility that allows each person to be the image of universal and timeless values. With this robbery begins the "revaluation of all values" as well as the distortion of all meaning that Socrates predicted. No longer is freedom—difficult and tragic freedom—the space that the individual needs to practice acquiring human dignity; rather, it is the *loss* of that dignity to the idolization of the animal ideal: everything is allowed. Meaning is unknown; sense is replaced with goal. "Fun" and "tasty" experiences replace the knowledge of good and evil. Because the everlasting doesn't exist, everything has to be now, new, and quick. No one can know any better, so everyone is right. Everyone is the same, so what is difficult is undemocratic. Art turns into entertainment, and what or whoever is famous is important. Gracián's statement that material weight determines the value of gold but moral weight determines human value is turned upside down. Morality? To each his own morality! Matter is king, and of all the little gods parading around, gold is the supreme deity. What is good for gold is good for you. Therefore be marketable! Adapt! Anything that makes you richer is useful, and what or who is not fun, not delightful, is in fact useless, can disappear. Everyone for himself, and no one for us all.

It is this nihilism of the mass society that, like a cancer, attacks civilization, the connective tissue of the social order, and destroys it. What remains without this connective tissue is an unlimited number of separate individuals who seek to destroy each other in the end because they are no longer united by one universal value but are seduced by the idea of "I am free, so everything is permissible." To what extent Western society is overrun by this nihilism is anyone's guess. The more important question is: Where does this nihilism come from?

*   *   *

Integrity is the ability to acknowledge your responsibilities. After the war Albert Camus owed it to himself as an intellectual with an intellectual's responsibilities to recognize that the intellectuals who, like himself, came out of the school of nihilism were jointly responsible for the torrent of destruction that had flowed across the Occident. And this was because they had consistently undermined the foundation on which the dam of civilization was built: immortal, life-affirming values and the timeless distinction between good and evil. Hence his timid but confident contribution to the conversation at Malraux's: "Aren't all of us responsible for the lack of values? And shouldn't we be the ones to openly declare that we were wrong, that moral values do exist, and that from now on we will do all that is necessary to establish and clarify them? Wouldn't that offer a beginning of some hope?"

Even during the war he had written in the same notebook: "Can man alone create his own values? Therein lies the whole problem." The conviction he expressed in the presence of Malraux, Sartre, and Koestler was his answer to the question. No, for the sake of human dignity the free individual is not allowed to ignore universal, timeless values. Intellectuals in particular should resist this kind of nihilism. Not everything is allowed. Human freedom is in essence relative; it is subordinate to the immortal and never completely attainable ideal of human dignity. Furthermore, absolute freedom obliterates justice. There are transcendental absolute values that have priority and are obligatory for *everyone*. Whoever then still defends nihilism or relativism is a moral dwarf, powerless in the face of violence and mass murder.

Camus knew that the only thing that justifies the existence of intellectuals was their responsibility to the world of ideas and the nobility of spirit. As guardians of civilization, they had a primary responsibility to indicate what was best in human life and to defend it in the public arena, to pass on a knowledge of values, to provide insight, to make distinctions, to protect the meaning of words. Not that doing so would change the world all that rapidly, but much is already gained when it is made publicly clear that lies are lies and that there is no power or fame that can make a lie into truth.

When millions of people can "believe" in nihilism, the guardians of the cultural heritage have failed or, worse, have committed treason. They lament capitalism, commercialism, and superficiality, yet support these ways of life by continuing their chatter that nothing is timeless or universal because everything is relative. Don't ask: What is the right way to live? Just do what's fun and tasty. It's all up to you. You're ignorant? Never mind. Nothing matters; anything goes, you see. Don't make problems; life is easy. Don't be serious; a little irony, please. There are no distinctions, we don't make distinctions. Making distinctions is elitist. And elitism is wrong, for it isn't democratic and we are against that, for we are against fascism.

This is the betrayal of the intellectual heritage par excel-lence: nobility of spirit, the essence of human dignity. And sadly, intellectual integrity appears to be a highly elitist characteristic.

*　　*　　*

That hot afternoon in Piraeus, Athens's harbor, Socrates
and his friends have already come to see that when freedom is
made absolute, it is essentially perverted and can never be the
cornerstone on which the ideal society can be built. Absolute
freedom always results in injustice, and injustice in murder. It is
not freedom but justice that must be the cornerstone. But because justice cannot exist without wisdom, without insight into
goodness, truth, and beauty, the just society requires a leadership with knowledge of the highest values: "Unless philosophers become kings there can be no cessation of troubles for
the human race."

Essential to the twentieth century is the fulfillment of the
Socratic ideal: the philosopher becomes king, the intellectuals
obtain their so fervently desired political power. And as this
ideal gradually takes shape, Thomas Mann during those long
years of war writes his *Reflections of an Unpolitical Man* (1919),
in which he passionately resists what he calls "the politicization
of the spirit." Julien Benda publishes *Treason of the Intellectuals*
in 1927. His now-classic analysis of the betrayal of the intellectuals is based on a thought that Thomas Mann formulated, that
the world of the spirit should always remain independent.

The politicization of the spirit is nothing other than another
reduction of reality. Just as commercialization—the spirit
blinded by gold, that little god—can see the world only in
terms of profit and loss, so the politicized spirit can see only
the political interests of society. Humanity's division is as
old as humanity itself. There are always the rich and the poor,
the powerful and the powerless. What is just? Who is entitled
to what? Like humanity, the politicized spirit is divided, for it
can see with only one eye at a time. Its right eye looks through

the glass of "property" and sees primarily wealth, order, law, preservation, tradition, the past, culture, and the nation. The left eye looks through the glass of "lack of property" and sees poverty, disorder, injustice, renewal, the future, science, solidarity and the international.

Universal and timeless truth, goodness, beauty, and justice are reduced to historical, socially determined political views. They lose their universality because that which is historical and political always divides. For in social reality there are always those who work hard and those who do not work, families and those without family, our own people and others, our traditions and that which we do not understand, the rich and the poor, the powerful and the powerless. The politicized spirit fosters these distinctions and bases its values therein. What is good and what is evil? What is true and what is not? What is beautiful and what is ugly? These questions, which never before received a definitive answer, now have answers on the basis of a historical-social analysis that permits only one correct answer: that which the left eye sees or that which the right eye sees. Left or right, one or the other, is always wrong. No matter what, the answer is by definition political.

The world of the spirit is silenced. There is no need any longer for a wisdom and art that isn't always unequivocal, that creates doubt, is intangible, requires receptivity. There is but *one* view of what is "good" morality, "good" art, philosophy, literature, truth, the right way to live. The proprietor of this "wisdom" is the modern philosopher-king: party ideologue, pundit, leftist, or conservative thinker.

Time is running out. A historic task awaits the proprietor of the Final Answer *and* of political power: destroying evil (the opposing party) and establishing and protecting what is Good

for Humanity. Law will triumph, utopia will arrive. That is
why the Jewish-Catholic Communist in Davos Dorf challenges
his humanist adversary to a duel. Politics is supposed to save
humanity and whoever is against us. . . . Isn't a human sacrifice
justified for the sake of this infinite earthly bliss—the ideal
state!?

"Yes!" is the fully confident response of the politicized mind.
"You must be realistic. Nothing happens without struggle and
sacrifice. Think of the goal."

"No!" said Ivan Karamazov. Eternal harmony may never be
obtained at the cost of the tears of a single innocent, tortured
child.

"No!" said Albert Camus. They asked him why he of all
people, born and raised in Algeria, took such a passive position in 1957 with regard to his "homeland's" fight for independence. Camus: "I was and still am an advocate of a just Algeria
in which the Algerians *and* the French can live in peace and
on equal terms with each other. I have said repeatedly that
justice must be done to the Algerian people and that Algeria
should have a completely democratic government. I fell silent
from the moment that it was no longer the intellectual's task
to be heard because the chance was great that the intellectual's declarations would exacerbate the terror. I have always
condemned terror. I must also condemn a terrorism that
operates blindly, in the streets of Algiers, for example, and
that may some day strike my mother or my family. I believe
in justice, but I shall defend my mother before I defend
justice."

Politicized minds do not see concrete individuals who
are alive, who love, and who are loved. All they see are
abstractions: capitalism, communism, globalization.

Socrates knew that, satiated with freedom, the "democratic person" would effortlessly surrender to dictatorship. Nodding in approval, Nietzsche knew it, too. The religious Communist in Davos Dorf saw the desire for absolute obedience as a sign of the times. The extremely erudite scholars in Munich were eagerly looking forward to the time when democracy with all its freedoms would come to an end.

In the same discussion where Camus offered his view on justice, he also expressed himself on the meaning of freedom. These were the days of the Cold War at its height, and the question arose, whether it was acceptable for a society that it-self lived with so much injustice to be critical of Russia, where there might not have been any freedom but where people were at least all equal. Camus: "A friend of mine who lost his life in the war against Nazi Germany said during the war: 'We are fighting a lie in the name of a half-truth.' He thought of himself as a pessimist, but were he still alive today, he would have come to the conclusion that we are once again fighting a lie but now in the name of a quarter-truth. It is that quarter-truth that we call *freedom*. But freedom is the way, the only way, to a more dignified human society. You can develop and perfect smoke-stack industries without freedom. But not justice or truth." Nobody needed to tell Camus about the shortcomings of the "West." But the experience of totalitarianism had taught him that human dignity would never stand a chance without human rights and constitutionally rooted and protected democratic freedoms. Without the freedom to think differently, speak dif-ferently, be different, have differences of opinion—without these freedoms, all other values are defenseless. And whatever one might think of the capitalist West, these freedoms are back again. Right here.

Freedom and truth do not exist without each other. Increasingly irritated with Sartre, who, blinded by his own political absolutism, wanted to keep the lie alive—"You have to be realistic; it is the goal that matters"—Camus wrote to a friend: "Sometimes I detest the times in which I live. I'm not an idealist. And it is not the realities, no matter how loathsome and cruel they may be, that I detest. It is the lies that are told about them. Confined by watchtowers, Russia is now a country of slaves. I shall fight to the end the idea that this concentration-camp regime is worshipped as the instrument that is to establish freedom and as a training ground for future happiness. . . . Only one thing on earth seems to me to be a greater good than justice—and that is, if not truth itself, the pursuit of truth. We don't need hope, we just need truth."

*   *   *

"Aren't we all responsible for the lack of values? Shouldn't we be the ones to openly declare that we were wrong and that moral values do exist?" That thought never left Camus again. Neither "society's interests" nor "historical necessity" could release him from his intellectual responsibility to serve civilization, to reason candidly, and to speak the truth. Together with Thomas Mann and Julien Benda, he came to see that the politicization of the spirit is also a kind of nihilism. The individual is no longer a spiritual being with questions to which no answer is forthcoming. The question about the meaning of life is replaced by the goal. The goal is happiness, and politics will provide that. No worries, no doubts, no questions. Myth or reason, tradition or science, right or left: one or the other will show the way—the way to the perfect society and the perfect human being. But the nobility of spirit has been cast out. The perfect barbarians have arrived.

*   *   *

Anyone devoted to civilization and intellectual life looks at twentieth-century European history in utter bewilderment. How many academics, writers, poets, artists, scientists, simply pushed civilized life aside to line up behind the triumph of the lie, dictatorship, and violence? How many scholars placed their intellectual talents in the service of the justification of terror? We don't dare to count them all. The list is endless. And how many servants of the spirit did *not* renounce their integrity and therefore lost their lives in death-and-prison camps, that hellish creation of an immense spiritual betrayal? That, too, is an endless list, rendering us speechless.

Let's have a look around. How many intellectuals are there today who consider that having the political Final Answer is more important than speaking the truth and reasoning without prejudices? "A crisis becomes a disaster only when we respond to it with preformed judgments, that is, with prejudices," Hannah Arendt concluded after the war.

The lack of intellectual integrity is enormous, as is the betrayal of the intellectuals. Are the failings of Western civilization any surprise? Why? Why this nihilism? Why this betrayal of the nobility of spirit?

The seductiveness of power is a first reason: to be influential at last, to be listened to at last, and, preferably, to be admired as well. Nothing is as addictive as power and fame. And to hold on to this, to maintain the position of party ideologue or pundit, to be the spokesperson of the "public," one needs continuously to adapt. If there is any place where conformity reigns, it is among politicized intellectuals. The idea of risking the loss of power and influence because of intellectual independence fills these realists with horror.

For the sake of political power they abandon the world of the spirit. The excuse is that the world needs to be changed, not interpreted. An end to injustice! But, as Benda in his treatise on the betrayal of the intellectuals correctly notes, great thinkers like Erasmus, Spinoza, and Kant have always remained faithful to the world of the mind as well as to their own independence. They did not nurture the arrogance of thinking that they could set humanity free from all evil, but they did remain true to their duty, which allowed the consciousness of what is good to exist. Knowledge of good and evil, an awareness of values and dignity, was safeguarded. Is that not sufficient justification to live life as an intellectual? For many intellectuals it is not: "Today, a special temptation of writers is that they can live largely by giving views about subjects of which they know nothing," Stephen Spender stated in 1951. Has anything changed since then?

A second reason for the infidelity to immortal values and nobility of spirit is bad faith. Some intellectuals do not believe in these qualities themselves. The immense influence of the scientific paradigm plays an important role in this. Immortality, meaning, value, good, evil, beauty, love, compassion, wisdom, justice, experience, virtue, and self-knowledge are words that do not exist in the language of the sciences. Theirs is the language of objectivity, facts, analysis, goal, progress. When the intellectual realm is constrained by this meaningless language, the spirit loses the ability to express meaning. Facts in and of themselves mean nothing. The *truth* of reality can come only through the knowledge of values, of the distinction between worth and worthless, good and evil, meaningful and meaningless. That is cultural knowledge, embedded in the language of artists, poets, and thinkers. This language is unknown to the pseudo-scientific intellectual clones. That is why they write so badly. With the exception of news from the world of "social reality," they have nothing worthwhile to proclaim.

And then we have "The Veiled Image at Sais." In this poem Schiller describes a young man who, driven by a yearning for absolute knowledge, travels to Sais, in Egypt, to seek instruction from the priests. "What do I know," says the youth, "if I don't know everything?" They go off to a temple containing a statue that stands behind a veil.

"What is hidden behind that veil?" the inquisitive young man asks.

"The truth," says the priest.

"Only a veil separates me from the truth?"

"Yes, a veil and the statue's command that no mortal 'will ever see me.'"

The priest departs. The young man stays. He looks—and is found dead.

This is one of the most ancient themes in the history of knowledge. The absolute truth and everything that is symbolic of it—the Holy Grail, the Knight of the Swan, the apple in Eden, the statue in Sais—you should not ask for it, nor look at it, nor try to possess it. The absolute is not for any mortal. "Woe to him who treads through guilt to truth / It shall never be a delight to him" is the poem's closing line. The sin of guilt is always pride. And what always follows is the fall. The youth dies alone. But the owners of the Final Answer and other fundamentalists never die alone.

*   *   *

Socrates! Where are you?

Socrates is with his friends and has not finished yet, for his friends don't give much credence, either, to the position that the philosopher should be king. They know too many intellectuals. But Socrates explains that only the *true* philosopher can be king because of having by nature a "good memory, quick apprehension," being "magnificent, gracious, friendly," and knowing "truth, justice, bravery, and sobriety." Fine, his friends object, in theory the state should obviously be led by this *honnête homme,* but the facts prove otherwise. Most intellectuals are, frankly speaking, corrupt. And society considers those who do have the characteristics with which Socrates endows his true philosopher such eccentrics that they could not possibly obtain any leadership position. Socrates wholeheartedly agrees. However, his life's purpose, to know wisdom, is discredited foremost by those who are professionally engaged in it: "They make a lot of noise in public, and without actually knowing what is good or evil, just or unjust, they use all these terms in agreement with what the masses, that great beast, seem to think about them: whatever pleases the beast is good, and what displeases it is bad. With this hollow talk, full of pretension and self-importance, always focused on what the masses want to hear, these people gain all the power. And the real authority on wisdom, the one who leads a life opposite to the needs of the masses, is deserted, lonely, and neglected."

He knew it. He knew that the true philosopher could never be king. He knew that the perfect society would never exist, and that there would never be an end to the ills that torment humanity. He knew that the true philosopher could only be a model.

Socrates, the eccentric, the friend of immortal values and of the nobility of spirit, was put to death in the prime of his life by the political powers that be.

Epilogue

And what about us? Are we still searching for the nobility of spirit?

Don't look for it in the world of the media, the world of politics, the world of noise. The spirit was never there. Don't go to academia. They have expelled the spirit. And the churches? There is a reason they sound hollow. The world of fame? There we would go astray.

In an old European city, the poet, ninety years old and shackled to his bed but with a mind that is still clear, hears that his dearest woman friend has died. Czeslaw Milosz writes:

What did I learn from Jeanne Hersch?

1. That reason is a great gift from God and one should trust in its capacity to know the world.

2. That they were mistaken who undermined confidence in reason by enumerating its determinants: the class struggle, libido, the will to power.

3. That we should be aware of being imprisoned in our perceptions but should not therefore reduce reality to dreams, illusions, produced by mind.

4. That truthfulness is a proof of freedom and falsehood is typical slavery.

5. That the appropriate attitude in the face of existence is reverence, and this is why one should avoid the company of those who debase it through sarcasm and who praise nothingness.

6. That—even if this shall lead to an accusation of arrogance—intellectual life governs itself by the rule of a strict hierarchy.

7. That the addiction of the twentieth-century intellectuals is *le baratin*—chatter devoid of responsibility.

8. That in the hierarchy of human activities art shall be placed higher than philosophy but that a bad philosophy can corrupt art.

9. That there is objective truth; out of two conflicting statements one is true, the other false, except in the cases when contradiction is legitimate.

10. That independently of the fate of natural religions one should conserve a "philosophical faith," e.g., the belief in transcendence as an important ingredient of our humanity.

11. That time condemns to oblivion only these works of our hands and minds that do not help—century after century—to build up the great house of civilization.

12. That in our own lives we should not despair because of errors and sins; the past is not closed, it receives meaning from our present actions. (Translated by Adam Zagajewski)

For us this is a didactic poem, a paean to the nobility of spirit. An eccentric woman. She would never be queen. She was a true philosopher.

Be Brave

I

The prosecutors have finished speaking and the accused has the floor. In the court of justice, located at the southern end of the marketplace, five hundred men have assembled to pass judgment on the seventy-year-old man who has risen to present his defense. When the old man passes a silent eye over the jurors seated before him, a hush falls over the room. The only sound heard is the chirping of birds, who are wholly indifferent to the seriousness of what is taking place inside the courthouse this early spring morning. All those present are acutely aware that this trial is vastly different from any other trial and that what is happening here will in all likelihood be discussed for generations to come. At the same time, even if none of them would openly admit it, the members of the people's court suspect they will be no more than nameless extras in the life story of the old man who stands silently watching, so poised and calm, his arms folded across his chest, as if he wants to demonstrate that what he has to say is far more significant to him than the death sentence his audience may well pronounce. His silence continues, and no one dares break it.

In the tense quiet with every eye upon him, memory inevitably returns to that cold winter morning more than thirty years ago. Almost everyone now present in the courtroom, including the accused, had gathered outside the city walls to listen to an oration they immediately knew should never be forgotten. The war was a year old, and according to custom, the Athenians who were the first to fall in battle were given a state funeral by their fellow townsmen. At the end of the ceremony Pericles, their leader, mounted a podium and addressed the crowd. His eulogy became a panegyric to Athens—a city that had the courage to be a democracy, where citizens coexisted in freedom and mutual tolerance. Respect for ancestors and traditions go hand in hand with a mind that is open to new developments and to giving every free citizen an opportunity to grow into an independent individual. It was a society in which people loved beauty without being wasteful and respected wisdom without being weak. Athens, thus said Pericles, was a training ground for the rest of the world. That is why Athens had to be defended, that is why the men who died for the city would never be forgotten.

Although an icy wind had risen during his speech, nobody felt the cold. Everyone went home filled with pride, and rarely would anyone speak of Athens again without reference to what they had heard on that occasion: we are the citizens of a society that is the model for other states; we represent the standard against which others will have to measure themselves.

Everyone had heard Pericles' oration, everyone had been present at that historic moment, even if their age made it impossible. Because everything had been told so often in the smallest of details, nobody could imagine not having been present three decades earlier to hear their famous leader speak.

Now the same men are together again to sentence one of their number to death if necessary. Why? The accusation was made as follows: "Socrates is guilty of corrupting the minds of the young, and of believing in deities of his own invention instead of the gods recognized by the state; therefore we demand the death sentence." This was the heaviest of punishments, but the accusations were no less weighty.

The news of a trial against Socrates on the grounds of this indictment came as no surprise, and from that moment on, virtually every conversation in the city had to do with *the trial*. People had seen it coming. Socrates, because of his actions, had made more enemies than friends, especially among the city's most prominent citizens. Anyone who spoke with the members of the jury preceding the trial could rapidly determine that opinion was divided on how the actions of the accused should be dealt with. Those who considered the influence of Socrates fairly negligible and thought the trial would draw greater attention to his ideas, planned to vote against a sentence, but in general there was unanimity on the justness of the accusations.

Sympathizers of those who had initiated the trial against Socrates made the most of every opening to justify the charge. "There are *fundamental* values at stake—no more, no less!" they said with solemnity. "Socrates has just one aim: to sow doubt. Doubt about what is and is not important; doubt about the wisdom of the authorities; doubt about traditions dating from the time of our ancestors; doubt about what people should do with their lives. People are being made uncertain, and these are already difficult enough times." The last comment was always met with many nods, for these were indeed difficult times for Athens. The war lost against Sparta, the plague, the political upheaval—all had taken their toll. These things were better not discussed in public, which would foster new unrest, but everyone knew that the once-so-proud state was slowly but surely sinking into decay. Socrates' opponents continued: "By shamefully ridiculing our values, the authorities, our social position and prestige, Socrates is helping the enemies of our city. Socrates is always saying that wealth and politics are of no interest to him, how his own life is enough for him. But we shouldn't be misled. What he wants more than anything is to turn the social order on its head!"

The accusers received enthusiastic support, which made it all the more irritating when an occasional individual—one of Socrates' friends, who else?—thought it necessary to comment that if all of this were true, one question still remained: How was it possible that the Delphic oracle, which always spoke the irrefutable truth, had declared: "There is no man wiser than Socrates"? It was a tough question, as tough as the questions and conclusions that Socrates would put to them. But there is no time left for further reflection. The voice of the philosopher breaks the silence. Socrates has begun his defense.

*   *   *

Aristocles, a young man of twenty-eight—and thus, to his regret, two years too young to be a member of the jury—has succeeded in obtaining a seat in the public tribunal thanks to being the son of a prominent family. Because the relationship with his family has been difficult for years—so difficult that he prefers to keep a safe distance between them and himself— he would have preferred not to have used his family name to secure a place at the trial. Yet he would never have forgiven himself for not being present.

For Aristocles, the path his life would follow was once a

foregone conclusion. His family's wealth and power, his following in the footsteps of both his grandfather—for whom he had
been named—and his father by occupying an important position in Athenian politics, all of this was according to expecta-
tion and called for no further scrutiny. The obviousness of
this path was strengthened by his evident status as a favorite
of the gods: he possessed a sharp intelligence, was a gifted
speaker, was admired for his writing style—at a tender age
he had gained some fame for his poetry and tragedies—and,
as if there were no end to the divine benevolence, he was
known for his tall, athletic body and his control over his physical strength. In short, there was no reason for doubt, not
about himself nor about the life that awaited him.

Then, eight years ago, Aristocles had first heard the old
man speak or, rather, pose questions—the same man who now
stands ten steps away from him in the middle of the crowded
room. Aristocles had not joined the conversation then, had
merely listened. When he walked home alone that evening, he
had asked himself questions he had never asked before. Why
be wealthy? Why seek a political career? Why comply with the
expectations of your family? Why? Why? And while this nasty
little word continued to echo inside his head, his carefree existence, once so neatly constructed of certainties and so taken
for granted, was slowly ripped apart by doubt.

That night Aristocles did not sleep, and as soon as dawn
broke he went to see Socrates. In answer to the latter's surprised question about the purpose of his visit at such an hour,
the young man could say only that he had made a decision.

"I want to change my life. I want to be your student."

"Young man, I am deeply honored, but I regret having to
disappoint you. I am no teacher, so I have no students. I

wouldn't even know what to teach you, because I don't know anything myself."

"As far as I'm concerned, you know everything."

"You are wrong. But you've aroused my curiosity. What is it you want to learn?"

Aristocles, completely surprised by Socrates' response, hesitated a moment, then, in a voice that was unable to hide his disappointment, said: "Socrates, my family is affluent, powerful, famous, respected by all, and until last night it was obvious to me that I would lead a life like others in my family. You have deprived me of what seemed so obvious to me. Can you imagine what it means to have everything you ever believed in, everything you always considered important, vanish right before your eyes like a sandcastle washed away by a single wave, all of it gone in one sleepless night? Have you ever sensed the void that comes with the disappearance of everything that once filled you with pride? Do you know the pain and disillusion that comes when you can no longer deny you have lived in nothing but a world of delusion?"

"Oh, I've made you unhappy, and now I'm supposed to restore your happiness—is that why you're here, disrupting the early morning quiet?"

"Please, no irony. You know I'm not here to complain. I may have been foolish enough not to recognize my complacent little world for what it is, but am not so foolish as to want to remain in it. It's high time for me to get to know the real world."

"I won't deny that, but it isn't me you should be seeking out. May I remind you that there's still a war raging? Go there, if only because there's no shame in fighting for your city."

Aristocles went. He returned three years later.

"Tell me" was all that Socrates said when they saw each
other again. Aristocles recounted the battles and his discovery,
heroic epics notwithstanding, that in the end war was nothing
more than the stink of rotting corpses, mutilated bodies,
and the dull sadness of the survivors. Indeed, his best-beloved
friend had been killed in battle. Now he had felt the piercing
pain of loss and pondered the ever-returning question about
the meaning of life when the very best can so easily vanish. He
had experienced loyalty and betrayal, had encountered brave
and cowardly people, and each time it was clear that neither intelligence nor affluence could provide any assurance of nobility
of spirit. Owing to his celebrated lineage, notable families had
welcomed him. He had partaken of sumptuous dinners, for
even in wartime such people lack for nothing. And yet, behind
the glow and laughter, there was nothing but a chilly, gaping
void, or so it seemed. He encountered rulers, and it was soon
apparent that the fine language about the "value of our traditions," "what is best for the people," the "common good"
had no other significance than that it served the interests of
his table companions. It struck him how readily people were
seized by passions and desires and what destructive power
these could contain. Revenge, hatred, jealousy, and violence—
every right-minded person is against them, but no one seems
capable of resisting their appeal. It appeared that people were
willing to believe anything and preferred that to careful reflection. However, what had impressed him most of all was the
omnipresence of the self-satisfaction that had so markedly
dominated his own existence: he noted the power of traditions
and "normality"; the seductive ease with which one adapts to
trends, opinions, and the established order; the uncontested
belief that everything is the way it is. The cherished longing

for an idle existence has as a consequence that awe of all that exists, and critical questions are seen not just as strange but as downright undesirable.

"Socrates," Aristocles said, "because of my build, my physique, the friend I lost always called me Plato, 'the broad-shouldered one.' I left as Aristocles to discover how the world really is. I have returned as Plato to learn what the world should be."

"Plato, dear friend, come here and let me embrace you. Now do you understand why you first had to abandon your family, your books, and me as well, and join that damned war? That you first had to become familiar with life before you could understand it? If you want to understand life, if you want to find a true answer to the question of what the right way of life is, then before anything else, this must become the vital question of your life, one that burns within like an inextinguishable passion. But as long as it is no more than a dutiful phrase, your existence will be nothing but the uncritical acceptance of the expectations of your family and your community, or else an obedient adjustment to the prevailing mores and customs. But if, now that you have seen so much senselessness, the question of what is really meaningful has become inevitable; if, once you have known pale desolation, you seek true consolation; if you are conscious of having lost what is dearest to you and the question of what still makes life worth living arises in silent despair, and, at the same time, you comprehend how empty the fine words are that priests spew, how hollow all complacency is, how pointless the existence of the mighty so frequently is, how you can be extremely erudite and still completely ignorant; if you know the deep-seated fear of perceiving when you are old that you have wasted your life with all sorts of things it again that you exposed as an extraordinarily erudite feather-brain? Euthydemus! It's undeniable that he had read so much in his early years and thought he'd learned so much that he really believed he was prepared to lead the city. Then you asked him two questions: "If you have read every book there is but you do not know yourself, what do you know? And if you are in command of all the scholarship in the world but you do not know the people, what are you capable of?" True, at least Euthydemus had the courage to learn from these questions and subsequently came to listen to you on a regular basis—which cannot be said of many of those who are here today to decide your fate. That is why this insane trial will lead to your death. You know that and I know that. For they won't forgive you, Socrates. They won't forgive you for exposing as ignorance the wisdom for which they pride themselves; for revealing that what is promulgated in this city as important turns out, after a discussion with you, to be not so important after all. They constantly use big words such as "bravery," "piety," "justice," but when you question them, it becomes painfully clear that they do not know what they are talking about. These people believe that to be civilized it is sufficient to live in the same city as Pericles and to parrot him. And then there you are to point out that this is not so. The question you never cease to pose and of which all your other questions are merely variations, that ostensibly simple and seemingly innocent question: So what, then, is the right way to live? is dreaded, thanks to your continued interrogations, and they would very much like to forbid its being posed. When you make them seek an answer to your question, too much of their cherished existence loses its justification. The prosecutors and their cronies have hauled you before this court because you robbed them of one word. They can still do what they are doing and live the way they are living, but you have seized the predicate "good" from their actions and existence. Something isn't good solely because "I am accustomed to it," "this is what I was told," "it is pleasant," "we enjoy it," "it serves my interests." As soon as you began to give words back their meaning, the lie of a society was laid bare. You became their conscience, the personified memory of a different life, of the fact that a life that is not easy will be infinitely more meaningful than an idle existence. That is why you must not only die but be forgotten. Your existence is unacceptable. That is why, dear old friend, I shall devote the rest of my life—and may the gods protect me—to the memory of yours. What you taught, I will write. The way you are is how you shall be known. I write so that not only your soul but your words, too, will be immortal. Nothing will be lost, and our names will be forever joined. But now you stand there alone while I sit here among the people. Socrates, speak! It is time for your defense. Let your words be mine.

* * *

"I never coveted fame or power. I have no money—look at my clothes and meager possessions. Divine wisdom is not mine, nor do I preach a particular faith. Is that why hatred, slander, and envy were my lot long before this trial? What is the culpability of an existence consecrated to the pursuit of human wisdom?

"This is what I know. It is wiser to know what you don't know than to feign knowledge of something you turn out not to have. Posing the right questions provides greater insight into human existence than uncritically repeating answers that others give us. Words are what convey our existence. When words lose their meaning, our life, too, becomes meaningless and withers like a tree whose roots have died. Teaching is for other people, but I would have failed miserably if I had not stimulated you to reflect upon the meaning of wisdom, bravery, piety, justice, and the like.

"Was it not together that we came to the conclusion that wisdom is nothing but the union between life and thought, that our actions alone can demonstrate whether we are truly wise and understand something about life? A thoughtless life is not only foolish but evil, and the knowledge that teaches us *how* to live is by far the most important knowledge.

"We examined the meaning of the word 'brave' and learned that the essence of true bravery does not lie in heroic conduct toward others but in the courage to dare to be wise oneself, in the practice of justice and other virtues, and in unconditional loyalty to the quest for truth.

"My prosecutors call upon their piety, but I ask you: How pious is he who knows everything about the gods—I won't ask how—and submissively follows all the rituals but hates his fellow men? The charge states that I deny the existence of the gods, but I have never denied the existence of the divine. On the contrary, I have always argued for the divine origin of the human soul. And because gods are gods and people are people, only the soul can teach us mortals what is truth.

"Because we are humans and not gods, not one of us can ever completely know the truth. That is why we will have to seek it over and over again, every new day; and with everything we encounter we have to ask: Is this true or not? Is this worthwhile or worthless? Does this enhance our dignity or rob us of it? The truth requires us to distinguish between what is good and what is evil. But what is truth? What is good? What has meaning?

"The soul, as the source of all life, teaches us that everything that gives life is good and everything that kills is evil. Everything that has a soul is good and will live on; everything that lacks a soul is worthless and cannot survive. The spirited life is unforgettable; life without spirit deserves oblivion. The best is true and will remain, but that which turns out to be a lie will vanish like snow beneath the sun. Thus, the best existence is devoted to the quest for truth and the practice of virtue. Loving human wisdom is nothing other than making these distinctions over and over again and unconditionally choosing the truth.

"Long ago I chose to be loyal to the quest for truth. I would rather suffer injustice than commit it myself. I would rather die than engage in lying. For the soul does not tolerate injustice, and it tolerates no lies. It wants to live in truth or else it dies, and my life would be over even though I still existed.

"Therefore if all of you, gentlemen of the jury, now tell me: Socrates, we shall acquit you, but only on one condition, that you give up spending your time on this quest and stop philosophizing. If we catch you going on in the same way, you shall be put to death.—Well, supposing, as I said, that you should offer to acquit me on these terms, I should reply, gentlemen, I am your very grateful and devoted servant, but I owe a greater obedience to God than to you, and so long as I draw breath and have my faculties, I shall never stop practicing philosophy and exhorting you and elucidating the truth for everyone that I meet. I shall go on saying, in my usual way: my very good friend, you are an Athenian and belong to a city which is the greatest and most famous in the world for its wisdom and strength. Are you not ashamed that you give your attention to acquiring as much money as possible, and similarly with reputation and honor, and give no attention or thought to truth and understanding and the perfection of your soul?

"And if any of you disputes this and professes to care about these things, I shall not at once let him go or leave him. No, I shall question him and examine him and test him; and if it appears that in spite of his profession he has made no real progress toward goodness, I shall reprove him for neglecting what is of supreme importance, and giving his attention to trivialities. I shall do this to everyone that I meet, young or old, foreigner or fellow citizen, but especially to you, my fellow citizens, inasmuch as you are closer to me in kinship. This, I do assure you, is what my God commands, and it is my belief that no greater good has befallen you in this city than my service to my God. For I spend all my time going about trying to persuade you, young and old, to make your first and chief concern not for your bodies nor for your possessions, but for the highest welfare of your souls, proclaiming as I go: wealth does not bring goodness, but goodness brings wealth and every other blessing, both to the individual and to the state.

"Now if I corrupt the young by this message, the message would seem to be harmful, but if anyone says that my message is different from this, he is talking nonsense. And so, gentlemen, I would say: you can please yourselves whether you acquit me or not. You know that I am not going to alter my way of life, not even if I have to die a hundred deaths."

*   *   *

In the state prison of Athens, a month after the death sentence is pronounced, Socrates drains the cup of poison.

II

In the state prison of Rome, in February 1944, Leone Ginzburg is tortured to death by his Nazi executioners.

*   *   *

A meaningful life knows no coincidences, but neither is it without choice.

Leone Ginzburg is raised in Italy, the son of a Russian Jewish family who, because of the turbulent political situation, fled Odessa right after his birth in 1909. Bilingual, multitalented, and mature at an early age, he completes a translation of Tolstoy's *Anna Karenina* when he is eighteen. At the time he is also reading the voluminous memoirs of his countryman Alexander Herzen, *My Past and Thoughts*. Ginzburg recognizes Herzen as his spiritual father and decides to devote his life as an intellectual to the spirit, values, and cultural heritage of Europe. He drops his legal studies, takes up the study of literature, and, when he finishes his studies, teaches the Russian language and comparative literature at the University of Turin. In addition, he writes essays, establishes a publishing house together with two friends, is closely involved in the publication of the books, plans to bring out a history series, and becomes editor in chief of the journal *La cultura*. Why? The Greeks taught him that the essence of true culture is the cultivation of the human soul, and he sees it as his intellectual duty to have the best of the European spiritual heritage—cosmopolitan and encompassing many centuries—made accessible in the most accurate publications. Thanks to the texts he publishes from the world of thought and literary imagination, people can acquire insight and, possibly, gain familiarity with a certain human wisdom. Culture, Ginzburg knows, is the accumulation of the paths that people can tread in their quest for the truth about themselves and human existence. Out of his commitment to this truth, he makes the transmission of and contribution to European culture his life's work.

*   *   *

Italy, late 1920s. When Ginzburg takes up his calling, Mussolini and his Fascists are in power. Slowly but surely the country falls under the grasp of a regime in which wisdom must make room for absolute obedience. However, Ginzburg has learned from Alexander Herzen's life story that culture and liberty cannot exist without each other. Whoever destroys liberty destroys culture.

A native Muscovite born in 1812, Herzen leaves his homeland permanently in 1847, when the despot Nicholas I is in power, to devote himself elsewhere in Europe to what he sees as his life's mission: to struggle for liberty and dignity for all. But Herzen is shocked by the Europe he discovers. In April 1850 he writes from his hotel room in Paris:

"The old, official Europe that one can see is not asleep— it is dying!

"The last frail and sickly vestiges of its former life are scarcely sufficient to hold together for a time the disintegrating parts of its body, which are striving to combine afresh and to enter into new forms.

"At first sight, there is much that is still normal; things run smoothly, judges judge, the churches are open, the stock exchange hums with activity, armies manoeuvre, palaces blaze with light, but the soul of life has fled, everyone is uneasy at heart, death is at our elbow, and, in reality, nothing goes well. In reality there is no church, no army, no government, no judiciary. Everything has become the police. The police are

In response to a reactionary priest who reproached him for not having done enough to combat the dissolution and materialism of society, he writes: "When antimaterialism and monarchic principles prevail instead of liberty, will you then show us a place where not only will we be left alone but also they will not hang us, burn us, or quarter us, as is now happening to some extent in Rome and Milan, in France and Russia?"

Yet it is not the freedom of the lower middle class or the merchants to which Herzen is committed. In *My Past and Thoughts* he presents the following reflection: "As the knight was the prototype of the feudal world, so the salesman had become the prototype of the new world; 'gentlemen' are replaced by 'entrepreneurs.' . . . Under the influence of this petty *bourgeoisie* everything was changed in Europe. Knightly honour was replaced by accountant-like accuracy, elegant manners by social convention, courtesy by affectation, pride by prickliness, parks by kitchen gardens, palaces by hotels open to *all* (that is, all who have money). . . . The whole of morality was now that those without money had to produce by all means possible, but that those with money had to preserve and increase their possessions; the flag which is run up in the marketplace to show that trading may begin has become the banner of a new society. People have *de facto* become the appurtenance of property; life has been reduced to a perpetual struggle for money. . . . Everything that is European in the modern sense has two characteristics that clearly stem from this trading mentality: on the one hand, hypocrisy and underhandedness; on the other, exhibitionism and window dressing. Only displaying the merchandise from its best side; buying it for half the price; selling junk as fine goods; letting the form come before the essence; appearance instead of being; behaving decorously instead of well, keeping up external respectability instead of inner dignity."

Is he too grim? Too pessimistic? He receives this criticism from many of his friends and readers. He finds support, however, when he reads John Stuart Mill's book *On Liberty*. In his memoirs Herzen notes: "A month ago Mill published a remarkable book in defence of *freedom of thought, of speech and of the individual*. . . . Two centuries ago, Milton defended the freedom of speech against attacks from the power of government, against the misuse of power, and all that was noble and vigorous was on his side. John Stuart Mill has a very different enemy: he defends freedom not against an advancing government but against *society,* against *custom,* against the murdering power of indifference, against bigotry, against mediocrity. . . . The continual degradation of personality, of taste, of lifestyle, the emptiness of the things that interest people, their apathy, are to him an abomination. On closer inspection he clearly sees how everything has become superficial, standardized, trivial, worn-out, maybe more 'bourgeois,' but all the more banal for that. He sees in England (what Tocqueville observed in France) the creation of general, one-of-the-herd types. And, gravely shaking his head, he says to his contemporaries: 'Stop! Think! Do you not realize where things are going with you? Look, your soul is languishing away!'"

Culture cannot exist where there is no freedom; but where culture is banished, freedom is meaningless, and all that remains is arbitrary and trivial. The freedom that Herzen wishes to defend with heart and soul is the freedom that is capable of shaping the character of individuals, the freedom that enables people to cultivate their souls and become models of human dignity. It is on behalf of this freedom that he creates the Free

Russian Press in London and establishes the journal *The Bell.*
He describes the editorial purpose of the magazine as follows:
"Everywhere, in everything, to always be on the side of freedom, against injustice, on the side of knowledge, against super-
stition and fanaticism, on the side of people growing to full
stature, against reactionary movements—those are our goals."
In this mission statement Leone Ginzburg recognizes a concise
description of the European ideal of civilization. However, it is
to a different mentor, Socrates, that he owes the insight that at
the heart of all culture lies an attitude toward life, a personal
ethics, in which words can be meaningful only if they are con-
verted into actions, in which unconditional loyalty is devoted to
a never-ending quest for the only thing that can provide life
with meaning: truth. It is this attitude toward life that Socrates
called human wisdom and true bravery.

For centuries, the classical humanistic ideal of living in
truth was dominated by the notion that this would be best
realized through the *vita solitaria,* the withdrawn, lonely
existence, away from the world of power and the temptations
of society. But Ginzburg agrees with Herzen that a life like
this is nothing more than a lie as soon as such absolute values
as freedom and justice are endangered and, with them, the
survival of civilization. In addition to his cultural activities,
this is the reason why he becomes deeply involved in politics
and—together with his closest friends, among them Andrea
Caffi, Nicola Chiaromonte, and the brothers of his future
wife, Natalia Levi—is active in the anti-Fascist movement:
because Fascism is a lie that denies the fundamental values
of European civilization.

In the years that follow, Leone Ginzburg and his political
friends are faced with persecution, arrests, and imprisonment,

Is it his imagination or is it reality? He doesn't know, but his cell door opens and a priest dressed in a cassock but with a huge swastika on his chest enters and sits down on the little stool. Ginzburg is shocked to recognize the small, thin, middle-aged man who was once his colleague at the university. He can't remember his name and is also not sure of the department in which he used to teach. Theology? Philosophy? Perhaps it was history or art history—he simply doesn't know. In any event, it was someone he had always avoided, for no particular reason, even though he had noticed that the man himself was looking for human contact when they were both teaching. For some reason the priest had not aroused any great sympathy in him, so their association had remained distant, if not unfriendly. He'd had the impression that the man was not particularly liked by any of his colleagues, although everyone had the greatest respect for his intellectual abilities. There was no book that he hadn't read, and he'd had a phenomenal command of languages. He could even read Russian. Suddenly Ginzburg remembers a specific situation. In January 1934, Ginzburg had refused—one of the very few, it later turned out—to sign the oath of allegiance to the Fascist regime. When he was clearing out his office at the university because his presence was no longer desired, the priest had stopped by. He remained standing in the doorway, and all he said was: "We won't forgive you for this." Ginzburg had looked at him in surprise and asked: "And who is 'we,' and what won't you 'forgive'?" The uninvited visitor answered: "*We* are people like me, who understand that life's greatest wisdom lies in adapting, and what we won't forgive is your unwillingness to accept that." Then the priest—still wearing a Catholic cross on his chest—had looked at him in silence for a moment, turned around, and walked away. Be-right, Francesco Petrarch, in his unsurpassed letters. Seven hundred years ago, my friend. Seven hundred years. Since that time has there been even one period, or even one year, when this complaint wasn't made? Has any real progress been made in this respect? We know the answer. You are so high-minded where your beloved *truth* is concerned and, yet you do not countenance authority. Why this absolute need for *freedom* and *democracy?* Why? I do not understand that. Did you read Herzen's memoirs so selectively that you missed the following passage: 'Is anyone who respects the truth going to ask the opinion of the first stray man he meets? What if Columbus or Copernicus had put the discovery of America or the turning of the earth to the vote?' Well, any comment? And Plato, our divine Plato, was he not prophetic when he predicted that all democracy would end in tyranny? People cannot handle freedom; it makes their lives too difficult. When it comes to this, Dostoyevsky, in his books, merely copied Plato. Didn't it all come true? Did you see how millions cheered for our great leaders, precisely as the immortal Grand Inquisitor described it? Give the people freedom and it will lead to rampant misconduct. This will be followed by more clamoring for 'values and norms,' and the very next leader who is nominally gifted in the art of rhetoric will be idolized again. You yourself have seen it happen. What makes you think things will ever change?

"Why do you despise Fascism? Is your democracy really that much better? Will its leaders be any better than those of our Fascist utopia? I'm not stupid: we're going to lose this war. Another year, maybe two, but then this adventure is over. I have no problem with that. Our ideas will remain, people will learn from what we know. Mark my words: 'democracy will be restored across the globe' with a great sense of drama. And then what? We are the ones who invented the power of propaganda, of images, and the intoxication that comes from being part of the masses. We are the ones who have understood that people are more interested in appearance than in substance. Do you really think that even one political party could survive if it were able to ignore this truth? Do you really think that a politician who wants no part of this can still be successful? Pretty pictures and rhetoric—that, my friend, is our legacy, and no one will escape it.

"What I truly don't understand is how you can possibly think that democracy and your culture can coexist. The masses are not interested, because their heads want no questions and their bellies want to be fed. Politicians are not interested, for their power depends on the stupidity of the masses. And the truly powerful, those who have the money, are not interested, because culture costs money. Have you ever been in America? I have—nice people, *nice people,* but no culture. Believe me, fifty years after the restoration of democracy across the globe, culture will be banned. Commerce and money will reign supreme, and unless something is *market oriented, democratic,* and *efficient,* it won't exist. Your publishing house, your books, and your journal will be the first victims. And there, where books can still be found, they won't be read. *Everything* will have to be *new, sexy,* and *appealing.* That's what sells, that's what people want. Would you please just admit that democracy and culture *cannot* coexist? It was predictable, it was tried anyway, and it failed. So be it.

"So why this resistance of yours? Don't you see that our true enemy is the very capitalist system that you so despise? That we're the ones who began the battle against the omnipotence of money? That we're the ones who want to maintain values and standards against hedonism, and our traditions, our culture, our identity against Americanism? Fortunately, most intellectuals have understood that we're fighting against the degeneration of society and for the recovery of classical values. That's why so many of them turned to Fascism without objection to the loyalty oath. All right, so we demand obedience; on the other hand, we provide intellectuals with the opportunity to constitute a true elite again. Besides, how critical are our intellectual friends? Do you know anyone who is more ambitious or more eager for recognition and fame than the contemporary sophist who has nothing to offer other than a multitude of opinions?

"You want to improve the world. Did you ever notice that once they are in power, all revolutionaries, whether they are Jacobins or Marxists, want one thing only: more power? And did you ever notice that as soon as the poor of this earth acquire any money, they want only one thing: more money? More power, more money; more money, more power. People never have enough. Call it a law of human nature. A world where this law is not the rule is unimaginable. And there is no law that creates more violence than the law of greed. It can't be that difficult to understand. What I find far more difficult to understand—and I hope you can help me with this—is that the great thinkers who are your heroes, such as Socrates, Petrarch, Dostoyevsky, and Herzen, understood human nature so incredibly well and yet have drawn such wrongheaded conclusions. It is precisely because people are *not* good that you can never expect to see a better world.

"If the world cannot be improved—and surely these last decades will, I hope, have shown that this will never happen—then only one conclusion can be the right one: obey the ruling power; adapt, and try to amass as much power for yourself as possible. Doesn't it amaze you that a Catholic priest like myself is now wearing a swastika? Isn't the Roman Catholic Church the best institution to teach absolute obedience and the art of adaptation? Would a real priest continue speaking when the Holy Father says 'Silence!'? Could Fascism ever have had such an astounding success in this country if we priests hadn't been there to teach it to the people? There aren't that many substantive differences between Catholicism and Fascism. The Germans overdo it with their anti-Semitism. Judaism is not something that we have a problem with—I certainly don't. On the contrary, I've always greatly admired your intellectual tradition and your sense of being the Chosen People. I recognize myself in that. . . . Possibly, after the war, you'll secure your own state after all—finally, your own country. And you know what will happen then? You'll want *more* land! It's quite understandable to me, actually, although from a historical perspective, the thought is a bit backward. A modern country doesn't want more land; a modern country wants *new markets.* All foreign people deserve respect as long as they buy our stuff. Economic power—that is the power of the future, my friend.

"Let's bring this Socrates-style discussion to a conclusion and say that it cannot have been because of the world that you brought this terrible fate on yourself. Your life, too, should be too valuable for such a hopeless case as our world."

The voice falls silent. There is not even any sniggering. When the voice begins again, something has changed. Where it was flat and emotionless, words are now more emphatic, and the voice trembles as if disguising pent-up anger.

"Only one possibility remains. It's not the *world* that you're concerned about, it's merely *yourself.* What was it that Socrates said in his defense? 'Give attention and thought to truth and understanding and the perfection of your soul!' How melodramatic. You really believe that nonsense? I find that hard to accept, and yet it's the only explanation I can come up with for the life you led and the choices you've made.

"However, do you still remember the conversation between Socrates and the wise Callicles? How the one who is truly wise defies your philosopher? 'I, Callicles, plainly assert that he who would truly live ought to allow his desires to wax to the uttermost, and not to chastise them; but when they have grown to their greatest, he should have courage and intelligence to minister to them and to satisfy all his longings. And this I affirm to be natural justice and nobility. . . . Nay, Socrates, for you profess to be a votary of the truth, and the truth is this:—that luxury and intemperance and licence, if they be provided with means, are virtue and happiness—all the rest is a mere bauble, agreements contrary to nature, foolish talk of men, worth nothing.' Is this truth or isn't it? And may I modestly add that the best way to attain this happiness is through adaptation and obedience—in a democracy as well, especially in a democracy, my friend.

"We weren't present at the conversation between your hero and mine, but believe me when I tell you that all Socrates did was stammer an answer. Forget what Plato wrote—he simply wanted to make the old man's attitude look better than it really was. But even Plato can't escape the fact that time and again, Socrates has but one argument with which to oppose the irrefutable reality that even he cannot deny, nor wants to: the immortal human soul aspires to its divine origin—truth.

"Well, then, what now? In the first place, the 'divine' seems problematic to me when both you and I know that the only god that can conceivably exist is truly *omni-impotens.* And surely I may assume that you, too, have knowledge of Nietzsche, Darwin, and Freud, who, each in his own way, merely repeats what Callicles so correctly posited."

The voice grows louder, grimmer.

"Why, then, all this nonsense about a soul and divine truth! I know, I'll burn in hell if it's true. But the only hell there is, my friend, is here on earth—a hell from which I've managed to escape."

Briefly it is silent again.

"Leone, I have always wanted to ask you the following."

The voice is whispering now.

"Do you understand what it would mean if Socrates is wrong? Do you understand that your entire life, everything you've accomplished, would rest on nothing but one huge, ghastly error? That you are letting them torture you, and will soon die, only thirty-five years young, because you believed in something false?"

It is silent. The sound of a slamming door. All goes black before his eyes.

* * *

Suddenly another image fills his head. An early summer morning. In the glow of the first rays of the sun the fields of grain paint the distant hills an ever-deepening yellow. The village is deserted. He has kissed his two sleeping children and the newborn baby. He is ready to head for Rome, but his young wife insists that he at least drink his coffee. Shortly thereafter they are outside the door together, in front of the small house where they have spent three of their five married years. A stately blue heron flies by. She embraces him, gives him a kiss. "Be careful," she says softly. He looks into her eyes, smiles, caresses her short hair, and says: "Be brave." Then everything goes white.

Selected Bibliography

Goethe. *Faust, Part One.* Translated and with an introduction and notes by David Luke. Oxford World's Classics. Oxford: Oxford University Press, 1987.

Gracián y Morales, Baltasar. *The Oracle, a Manual of the Art of Discretion / Oráculo manual y arte de prudencia.* The Spanish text and an English translation, with critical introduction and notes, by L. B. Walton. London: Dent, 1953.

Herzen, Alexander. *From the Other Shore,* translated from the Russian by Moura Budberg, and *The Russian People and Socialism,* translated from the French by Richard Wolheim, with an introduction by Isaiah Berlin. Oxford: Oxford University Press, 1979.

Herzen, Alexander. *My Past and Thoughts.* 4 vols. Translated from the Russian by Constance Garnett; revised [and edited] by Humphrey Higgens; with an introduction by Isaiah Berlin. London: Chatto and Windus, 1968.

Mann, Thomas. *Doctor Faustus: The Life of the German Composer Adrian Leverkühn as Told by a Friend.* Translated from the German by John E. Woods. New York: Alfred A. Knopf, 1997.

Mann, Thomas. *The Magic Mountain: A Novel.* Translated from the German by John E. Woods. New York: Alfred A. Knopf, 1995.

Plato. *The Collected Dialogues of Plato: Including the Letters.* Edited by Edith Hamilton and Huntington Cairns. Bollingen Series LXXI. Princeton, N.J.: Princeton University Press, 2005.

Plato. *The Dialogues of Plato.* 3d edition. Translated into English, with analyses and introductions, by B. Jowett. Oxford: Clarendon Press / Oxford University Press, 1931.

Todd, Olivier. *Albert Camus: A Life.* Translated from the French by Benjamin Ivry. Alfred A. Knopf, 1997.

Whitman, Walt. *Complete Poetry and Collected Prose.* Edited by Justin Kaplan. The Library of America. New York: Literary Classics of the United States, 1982.

Author's Note

Next to "unforgettable conversations," there are unforgettable letters. One of them is the letter Niccolò Machiavelli wrote to his friend Francesco Vettori on December 10, 1513. In the letter he explains how he came to write his small but important treatise *The Prince*. The following paragraph is famous:

> When evening comes, I return home and enter my study; on the threshold I take off my workday clothes, covered with mud and dirt, and put on the garments of court and palace. Fitted out appropriately, I step inside the venerable courts of the ancients, where, solicitously received by them, I nourish myself on that food that alone is mine and for which I was born; where I am unashamed to converse with them and to question them about the motives for their actions, and they, out of their human kindness, answer me. And for four hours at a time I feel no boredom, I forget all my troubles, I do not dread poverty, and I am not terrified by death. I absorb myself into them completely. (Translated by J. B. Atkinson and David Sices)

I invited old friends from my own study to contribute to the writing of this book. If phrases and conversations seem familiar, they are: borrowed directly, courtesy of the publishers, editors, and translators who make them available. Other words are mine. Readers teased by an unquoted passage in the "Untimely Conversations" chapter will find it in chapter 34 of Mann's *Doctor Faustus*.

Readers who want to pursue other quotations or, even better, participate in unforgettable conversations like those mentioned in my book will find sources in the Selected Bibliography. Machiavelli is right: the best medicine to alleviate boredom, lighten the weight of troubles, and dim the dread of poverty and the fear of death is by spending at least four hours a day in conversation with masters from the world of philosophy and literature. As Socrates would put it more positively, thoughtful conversation is the best way to examine life and make it worth living.